Cleopatra and Egypt

Blackwell Ancient Lives

At a time when much scholarly writing on the ancient world is abstract and analytical, this series presents engaging, accessible accounts of the most influential figures of antiquity. It re-peoples the ancient landscape; and while never losing sight of the vast gulf that separates antiquity from our own world, it seeks to communicate the delight of reading historical narratives to discover "what happened next."

Published

Cleopatra and Egypt
Sally-Ann Ashton

Alexander the Great in his World
Carol G. Thomas

Nero
Jürgen Malitz

Tiberius
Robin Seager

King Hammurabi of Babylon
Marc Van De Mieroop

Pompey the Great
Robin Seager

The Age of Augustus, second edition
Werner Eck

Hannibal
Serge Lancel

In Preparation

Constantine the Great
Timothy Barnes

Julius Caesar
W. Jeffrey Tatum

Cleopatra and Egypt

Sally-Ann Ashton

Blackwell Publishing

BLACKWELL PUBLISHING
350 Main Street, Malden, MA 02148-5020, USA
9600 Garsington Road, Oxford OX4 2DQ, UK
550 Swanston Street, Carlton, Victoria 3053, Australia

First published 2008 by Blackwell Publishing Ltd

1 2008

Library of Congress Cataloging-in-Publication Data

Ashton, Sally-Ann.
Cleopatra and Egypt / Sally-Ann Ashton.
p. cm. – (Blackwell ancient lives)
Includes bibliographical references and index.
ISBN 978-1-4051-1390-8 (pbk. : alk. paper) – ISBN 978-1-4051-1389-2 (hardcover : alk. paper) 1. Cleopatra, Queen of Egypt, d. 30 B.C. 2. Egypt–History–332-30 B.C. 3. Queens–Egypt–Biography. I. Title.
DT92.7.A84 2008
932′.021092–dc22
[B]

2007037051

A catalogue record for this title is available from the British Library.

Set in 11 on 13 pt Bembo
by SNP Best-set Typesetter Ltd., Hong Kong
Printed and bound in Singapore
by C.O.S. Printers Pte Ltd

The publisher's policy is to use permanent paper from mills that operate a sustainable forestry policy, and which has been manufactured from pulp processed using acid-free and elementary chlorine-free practices. Furthermore, the publisher ensures that the text paper and cover board used have met acceptable environmental accreditation standards.

For further information on
Blackwell Publishing, visit our website at
www.blackwellpublishing.com

For my parents, Jacqui and Robin Ashton

CONTENTS

ILLUSTRATIONS

FIGURES

PLATES

AUTHOR'S FOREWORD

My aim for this project was to try to find the "real" Cleopatra. What I have subsequently realized and accepted is that by "real" I meant "my" Cleopatra. My presentation of the queen will inevitably reveal my own strengths and weaknesses as a writer and a scholar. Nevertheless, I hope that this book will present a different way of investigating a figure with whom many readers will feel a sense of familiarity. I consider my strengths to be as a Classical art historian/archaeologist and Egyptologist and as such I have relied heavily on the interpretation of these sources in order to attempt to understand how Cleopatra was presented. When I started writing I was determined not to rely upon the Roman written records as my main source of evidence, as others had done in the past, in order to provide a tidy historical narrative of Cleopatra's life. I soon realized that making reference to these sources was essential in order to fill in many gaps that the archaeology and scant documentary evidence from Egypt during her reign provided. I have tried to be mindful of the fact that these sources are biased and that their accuracy is, in many cases, questionable. I have also attempted to use the Egyptian sources as a framework on which to build and embellish rather than attempting to make the archaeological evidence match the Roman texts.

The order of the book has changed a number of times on account of the complexity of the archaeological sources and the different personas that Cleopatra adopted in Egypt, which changed according to her consort, the different aspects of her role as an Egyptian ruler, and the target audiences in the wider ancient world. I have worked on Cleopatra for almost ten years and find that the more I delve into her history, the more complex a character I find. My Cleopatra is by no means a straightforward or definable figure, but remains, I hope, a person of inspirational character.

Sally-Ann Ashton
Cambridge, 2007

ACKNOWLEDGMENTS

I would like to thank Robin Ashton, Ian Blair, and Susan Thompson for reading the initial manuscript, and for trying to make sense of it all. I am grateful to Emmanuel De Silva II and Mary Hamer, who commented on the early drafts of Chapter 1. The end product is much improved as a result of my discussions with both of them. I am extremely grateful to Dorothy Thompson for her comments on the book's content and final order; also for her encouragement. Any remaining errors are my own.

I would like to thank Ayman Wahby Taher for sharing his knowledge of the Temple of Hathor at Denderah and for taking the time to introduce me to the wealth of information contained there, beyond the South Wall. I have had many discussions with Bob Bianchi on the subject of Cleopatra and wish to acknowledge this beyond the simple references within the text. I am especially grateful for his thoughts on the building scheme at Denderah, some of which are reflected in the text.

Finally, I would like to thank Al Bertrand of Blackwell for his patience and encouragement throughout this project.

1

CLEOPATRA – BLACK AND BEAUTIFUL?

1.1 A TWENTY-FIRST CENTURY VIEW?

Anyone working on Cleopatra will frequently be asked two questions on the subject, namely "was Cleopatra beautiful?" and "was Cleopatra Black?", the latter most commonly expressed in the Eurocentric form of "Cleopatra wasn't really Black was she?" Although these questions are bound by modern expectations they are relevant to Cleopatra as a historical figure and deserve further consideration in the context of this book.

The simple answer to both questions with regard to Cleopatra is that we do not know whether she was beautiful and Black, unattractive and White or a combination of any of these modern concepts. We do not have the body to indicate her race through testing DNA; however, this missing link should not prevent the queen being seen as an African icon, and in fact the surviving archaeological evidence supports the idea that Cleopatra presented herself as an Egyptian. Cleopatra was of course descended from Macedonian Greeks, but by the time she first came to power in 51 BCE her family had lived in Egypt for 272 years. In addition to this fact we do not know the identity of Cleopatra's grandmother, who may have been a concubine rather than an official wife, and more recently the identity of Cleopatra's mother has been questioned (Huß 1990).

The aim of the present book is to place Cleopatra within an Egyptian context and to consider her as a ruler of Egypt, not as a Greek monarch. Re-adjusting to this way of thinking, beyond the Roman written sources on which people usually rely, poses similar issues to the question of Cleopatra as an African queen. The aim of this chapter is to challenge conventional European perspectives of Cleopatra.

Cleopatra's identity as an Egyptian rather than a Greek was clearly established during her lifetime. Immediately after her death Strabo describes the queen as "the Egyptian woman," as implied by the feminine form of the adjective Egyptian (*Geography* 13.1.30). Here Strabo describes how Antony raided temples for statues of a Greek hero and gods to gratify "the Egyptian." The second-century Roman Lucius Annaeus Florus described her as "That Egyptian woman" (*Wars* 2.21.1–3; Jones 2006: 106).

1.2 AFRICAN ICON

Cleopatra's ethnicity is a contentious subject and one that is often dismissed in academic circles. By chance I witnessed an example of such a discussion by visitors to the Metropolitan Museum of Art, New York in the summer of 2006. One of the museum's most imposing displays is of the small temple from Dendur. This temple is inscribed with texts and images that relate to the Roman emperor Augustus. I had studied the temple many times during previous visits to the museum, but was paying particular attention to the carved inscriptions in light of the preparation for this book. Whilst I was looking at the outside of the temple a father and his children stopped close to where I was standing. The man, who from his accent was American and from the conversation that ensued I assume was of Greek descent, said to his sons that in school they would be told that the Egyptians were the forefathers of African-Americans and that this was wrong. He asked his children if they thought the figures looked like African-Americans. The children shook their heads in agreement with their father, who said that they should remember that Cleopatra was queen of Egypt and that she was a Greek, as indeed were his sons' ancestors. The man was misinformed on two accounts. Firstly, the temple dates to the early Roman period, so why should the figures look African? Secondly, Cleopatra was not exclusively Greek.

I am not of African descent. Consequently, I cannot really fully understand the importance of claiming Cleopatra as an African queen. I have been fortunate to work with substantial numbers of members of British African-Caribbean communities, who have shared their views on Cleopatra's connection with Africa and with African cultural heritage. There is no denying that Cleopatra was queen of an African nation. Egypt is in Africa and many Africans from elsewhere on the continent believe Egypt to be part of their cultural heritage (O'Connor and Reid 2003: 1–23).

Many Egyptians today do not consider themselves part of Africa; they do, however, think of Cleopatra as an Egyptian monarch and she is shown as an Egyptian on a variety of products from the national brand of cigarettes and wine, to local tram and train stations (Walker and Ashton 2006: 23–7).

Irrespective of the tone of her skin color, the evidence for Cleopatra in Egypt strongly suggests that Cleopatra wanted to be seen as an Egyptian in her home country and that her Greek heritage was neglected in favor of native (Egyptian) tradition. Scholars who have questioned Cleopatra's cultural affiliation with Greece and supported her Egyptian (and so African) heritage have met with at best contempt and at worse the accusation that their arguments are unscholarly because they are influenced by their own cultural identity. This is because few white scholars have bothered to consider the importance of Cleopatra as a Black role model and icon. One Black American classical scholar wrote the following: "She [Cleopatra] represents the contemporary Black woman's double history of oppression and survival" (Haley 1993: 29). Haley chronicles how, as a Black American, she questioned the African-American cultural oral tradition of considering Cleopatra to have been a Black woman (1993: 28–9 and n.4). The motives of Black academics who draw upon their own cultural identity are frequently questioned by those who have no such claim. It seems that there is a deep-rooted suspicion of those who are deemed to have minority agendas, with some critics even attempting to find an explanation for what is perceived to be an individual's radical point of view (Bernal 2001: 206–8).

The very fact that it is necessary to defend even the possibility of Cleopatra's association with Africa demonstrates the extent to which both Classics and Egyptology have become Eurocentric in their core perceptions. I would, however, ask if we are, as Europeans, so keen to embrace the rulers of Dynasty 26, when Greeks settled at Naukratis, as part of Classical history? – Of course we are not; this would be preposterous. There is generally no need to defend Cleopatra's European heritage, even though the queen showed little interest in presenting herself as such (Ashton 2003d: 25–30).

Classical scholars have argued that Cleopatra's Greekness can be defined on the basis of her name; that she was of Macedonian ancestry; that her family had imposed itself on Egypt; and that her reported fluency in the Egyptian language did not make her Egyptian (Lefkowitz 1996: 4). Part of the problem seems to lie in the fact that few Classical scholars are able to understand or interpret Cleopatra's Egyptian persona. They cannot read the texts; all of the images appear to the standard Eurocentric training as the same and even when differences are explained to them, the Egyptian evidence is dismissed as Cleopatra paying lip service to the country that she ruled. This problem is not limited to Cleopatra. In fact for years classical scholars have ignored Egyptian aspects of Ptolemaic Egypt, presenting a wholly biased and false interpretation of this period in general. Many realize that they are at a disadvantage when working on a subject that is effectively split between two very different cultures and that there is a Hellenistic/Greek bias (for example Rowlandson 2003; Thompson 1988). Such scholars have contributed important scholarship to the subject and I am not for one moment suggesting that the Hellenic tradition should be forgotten, but rather that it is necessary to re-address the balance of scholarship. I do not blame my colleagues for this problem and feel wholly justified in raising the issue because of my own training, initially as a Classicist. This difficulty is wholly due to the way in which the subject is taught at university level. It is easy to fool oneself that one's own way of thinking is correct. After three years of studying Egyptian material culture and languages, I was forced to re-write the first two chapters of my doctoral thesis. Initially I had only taken account of how the Greeks viewed material culture and interpreted the sculpture that I was studying through a Greek perspective. Added to the usual bias is the fact that everyone views culture through what they have been taught and their own experiences, no matter how hard they try to do otherwise.

And so, the Eurocentric view of Cleopatra also extends to the study of her by classical scholars, many of whom have denied her Egyptian character. Until recently Cleopatra's Greek image was seen by many to be dominant (Kleiner 2005: 138–9). It seems incongruous then that Royster (2003), who criticizes the Eurocentric view of Cleopatra, missed the point of the 2002 Chicago version of the British Museum's special exhibition *Cleopatra of Egypt: from history to myth*. A substantial part of this exhibition was dedicated to Cleopatra's Egyptian persona and offered a number of newly identified images showing the queen as an Egyptian rather than the hitherto only classical representations (Ashton 2001b). The identifications had been made by following stylistic and iconographic changes rather than by comparing the classical "portraits" that appear on the coinage. Royster complains that Cleopatra as an African-American icon was largely absent from the exhibition (207–10), and is right to do so. However, her grievance, that Egyptian-style representations are deemed to be stylistic and Greek naturalistic (203), reveals a lack of understanding of ancient artistic conventions. The Cleopatra of Shakespeare or modern film is not the real Cleopatra.

Quite apart from the proposal that Cleopatra was even partly of African descent and so can, in turn, be considered as part of Black culture and history, there is another layer that is often ignored by the Afrocentrics and which would, in my opinion, strengthen their case, particularly if we consider Egypt to be part of a wider African civilization. Cleopatra was shown as an Egyptian both in Egypt and, on at least one occasion, in Rome. As noted, Roman historians frequently refer to Cleopatra as an

Egyptian and she was by no means welcomed into the European tradition that was Rome; in fact the contrary is true.

In some respects African-centered scholars do themselves no favors by using weak arguments to support what is actually a strong case for Cleopatra's presentation as an Egyptian. One example of this is that Shakespeare described Cleopatra as "tawny" and so Black (Clarke 1984: 126–7). In fact it doesn't really matter how Shakespeare saw Cleopatra, because he was not her contemporary. A glance at the queen's representations and images, however, demonstrates that Greece did not play any real part in her presentation at home in Egypt.

Roman writers may not refer to the color of Cleopatra's skin – would they have even noticed if she was a quarter African? Possibly not. This fact does not, however, belittle her appeal to a modern Black audience, and nor should it. So strong is the idea that Cleopatra was white and wholly European in her outlook that another weak argument is frequently used to counter the Afrocentrics: that no authors mention Cleopatra was Black and so therefore she must have been white. For example, Lefkowitz (1996: 22 n.2) wrote: "Who was the mistress [of Ptolemy IX]? Since none of the sources tells us otherwise, the natural assumption was that she was Greek, like the Ptolemies. That of course does not prove she was not African, but there is no evidence at all that she was African."

That a Black Cleopatra is a valid concept has been attacked on account of its acceptance by the African-American oral tradition, once again raising the question of whether the Roman written tradition can be seen to be any more reliable or valid (Palter 1996: 352). Although many scholars cite the lack of written evidence that Cleopatra was Black as proof of her pure European descent, there are other aspects of her life and character that are equally nebulous but which are generally accepted. Cleopatra was of course part Greek but it must also be noted that the suggestion she was part African is not based on wishful fantasy alone but on the fact that we do not know the identity of the mother of Ptolemy XII and so Cleopatra's paternal grandmother.

Few historical figures have provoked such a struggle by others to claim them as an ancestor. Perhaps the most alluring point of Cleopatra is that she brings European and African cultures together. As a woman of Greek origin, possibly part Egyptian, who chose the latter culture with which to associate herself, we have a more remarkable role model for modern society.

1.3 EGYPT AND AFRICA

The question of Cleopatra's African identity is bound tightly within the question of Egypt as part of Africa. This exemplifies the contrast between Black history/identity and Classical/European identity and reflects the European appropriation of African culture. The question of Cleopatra's color and ethnic identity features in a number of publications on Egypt's influence on Greece and Egypt as part of African cultural heritage. Scholars tend to argue strongly for or against the idea that Egypt is African (for example Lefkowitz and Maclean Rogers eds. 1996). However, as many strive to deny this association in the case of Cleopatra, others use her mixed origins as proof that the contamination of the Macedonian bloodline led to the Dynasty's downfall (Bianchi 2003: 13).

In North America some people with a trace of African heritage consider themselves to be Black and there is the wider use of the term Black in contemporary Britain to include [South sic.] Asian communities (Bernal 2001: 209). A recent exhibition on Black Victorians (Marsh 2006) included images of people of Islamic origin. Bernal has pointed out that to modern Europeans Black means a "Stereotype of west Africans" when Africa, including North Africa, is very diverse. I labor this point in order to illustrate how we are dealing with semantics. It is however unfair of scholars to say that being African versus Classical (European) was not an issue in ancient times. When representing Amasis, the Egyptian attendant of Memnon, the fifth-century-BCE Athenian potter Exekias showed the figure as a Black African, with Afro hair and exaggerated "African" features. It has been suggested that this was also a reference to a rival potter who was working in Athens at this time. Thus to the Greeks an Egyptian could be an African. In Greek literature Egyptians were often referred to as Ethiopians.

It is also important to accept that ethnicity is not only about the degree of color or culture; it is also about choice. Thus children who are of mixed race often decide to follow a dominant culture; generally Black–White becomes Black, partly because in terms of a physical appearance (color of skin and hair type) people with Black/White parents are usually closer to their Black parent in appearance, and so are treated as such by society at large. Black culture also has a great appeal; many people in Britain today follow or imitate Black culture (music, film) but are not Black. Cleopatra had two very different images. The first and dominant was her Egyptian image and as ruler of Egypt Cleopatra embraced her native culture (her family, it must be remembered, had lived in Egypt for almost 300 years at the time of her accession to the throne). Cleopatra was only shown as a European when her audience necessitated it and yet Europe still appropriates her as one of its own, ignoring the African connection.

1.4 CLEOPATRA AS A ROLE MODEL

There are few women who can match Cleopatra's prominence, or who have wielded her power. As a consequence, many modern writers look to Cleopatra as a feminist icon, while others do their best to undermine this role.

Cleopatra as a role model for women is as problematic as Cleopatra as a Black icon. There is a simple explanation for this problem and, arguably, one that might offer insight into the need to comment on her physical appearance. The majority of Cleopatra's biographers and certainly the majority of ancient historians who include her in their work were men of European origin. Chapter 2 will evaluate this problem by comparing ancient North African writers with their European counterparts.

Modern historians who work on African history and identity or who are of African origin are more sympathetic to the idea of Cleopatra as a Black icon, perhaps because they are familiar with the African-American oral tradition. It is perhaps of no surprise that female historians deal more sympathetically with the queen and in particular those who specialize in the "myth" of Cleopatra, perhaps quite simply because they realize just how distorted her character has become over time (especially Hamer 1993 and 2003; Hughes-Hallet 1990).

Scholarship cannot question Cleopatra's gender in the same way that it has questioned her cultural identity but some scholars have queried Cleopatra's place as a role model for women. Cleopatra does not have to be infallible as a historical figure to fulfil this function, in the same way that her own or the modern perception of her color is not relevant to Cleopatra's acceptance as a Black icon. If some members of two "minority" groups (and I include women here) can look to Cleopatra, an inspirational historical figure, as a role model why should this bother those who have no perceived claim upon her? I am not suggesting that Cleopatra was infallible, but it would be wrong to deny modern affinity to her, be it female, Black, or Egyptian.

1.5 ATTITUDES TO FEMALE RULERS

Some modern scholars, when considering Cleopatra VII's track record as a ruler, cite natural disasters such as the low floods during the early part of her reign as examples of the queen's poor management of Egypt. In a remarkable conclusion one (Hazzard 2000: 159) wrote: "The Ptolemaic queens provide no shining examples to feminists if they judge them by their own values, for the emergence of these queens hardly improved the quality of government or bettered the condition of their own sex. And this is particularly true of the last Cleopatra, now more of a legend than a historical figure. Ignoring her brother's rights in 51 (to rule), serving her Roman patrons throughout her reign, killing 3 claimants to the throne and extracting large tribute from her people, the last Cleopatra emerged greater than her male associates, but ruled with the cruelty equal to any king's."

Although some modern historians seem to struggle with the concept of a strong female figure-head, women had played a key role in Egypt from the time of the First Dynasty and clearly filled a specific role that was closely connected to influential goddesses. Egypt had been governed by female rulers but their status was far from the norm. In an essay on models of (female) authority in regard to the accession of Hatshepsut, Roth has considered the circumstances surrounding the promotion of women to the position of principal ruler (2005: 9–14). Many women came to power after an untimely death of their consort. Others held power, but not the title of King, as regents and King's mother (Roth 2005: 10–12). Egyptians clearly accepted and accommodated female rulers, and women were seen to be capable of protecting Egypt, and they might be buried with objects associated with military bravery (Roth 2005: 11). This is of little surprise when one considers goddesses such as Sekhmet, who had both protective and warring sides to her personality.

The Greeks had an equivalent to the lion-headed Sekhmet: Athena. In Classical Greece female warriors were limited to the realms of mythology. There was no Greek equivalent to the office held by Egyptian royal women. However, in Macedonia at the time of Alexander we see a very different type of woman emerging. As in Egypt women were used to cement political allegiances. Philip II of Macedon, Alexander's father, took a total of seven wives but divorced none. Philip's wives and his daughters were warriors who went into battle, arranged their own daughters' marriages and promoted their sons (Ashton 2003a: 14). Alexander had a particularly strong and powerful mother who, following his death, did all she could to preserve her own position, including placing her statue alongside that of her deified son in a family shrine at Olympia in Greece (Stewart 1993: 386–7). It was following this particular Macedonian model that the early Ptolemaic queens sought to increase their power. By the second century BCE they actively sought to promote their position, often at the expense of their consort.

During the Ptolemaic period there was even a straightforward mother and daughter rule. Cleopatra Tryphaina, consort of Ptolemy XII (Cleopatra VII's father) and their daughter Cleopatra Berenice IV ruled from 58–55 BCE. It is in fact here where the confusion over the number of Cleopatras occurs. Porphyry refers to Cleopatra Berenice as the sister and not the daughter of Cleopatra Tryphaina, which would create a second Cleopatra Tryphaina and a sixth Cleopatra (Ashton 2003a: 67–8). There is little evidence to support another female named Tryphaina and it is likely that Porphyry was confused (Whitehorne 1994: 182–3). The queen we know of as Cleopatra VII is actually Cleopatra VI. To avoid further confusion she will be referred to in this publication simply as Cleopatra or with her usual number.

The Romans were not quite so comfortable with the idea of a female ruler. On several occasions they intervened to put a male ruler back on the throne in place of a woman. Their most disastrous intervention was the marriage of Cleopatra Berenice who had ruled with her uncle Ptolemy X and her father Ptolemy IX and was then given sole charge of Egypt upon her father's death. Cleopatra Berenice ruled for six months before the Romans selected her nephew to rule with her; within weeks she was murdered by her husband. The Alexandrians took their revenge and killed their new king.

1.6 CLEOPATRA'S BEAUTY

On February 14th, 2007, the tabloid press in Great Britain ran articles with titles such as "Cleopatra the Minger." Even the broadsheet newspapers included articles on the question of Cleopatra's beauty. The stimulus had been the University of Newcastle Museum, which had found a coin of a relatively common type and put it on display for Valentine's Day.

It is easy to dismiss questions regarding Cleopatra's beauty (Hamer 2003: 126). Nevertheless, the subject deserves further consideration. Coin images (Plate 1.1) are used against the queen's alleged beauty quite simply because they do not conform to the

Plate 1.1 Coin showing portrait of Cleopatra VII on the obverse and Mark Antony on the reverse, minted in Antioch in 36 BCE. The Fitzwilliam Museum, Cambridge, inv. CM.LK.864-L and CM.6.300-1933

modern Western concept of what is acceptably attractive. Few male historical figures have to suffer the same indignity of being judged on one image that has been deemed to be unflattering. A quick look at Cleopatra's other images reveals a type that is dramatically different to the later coin "portraits" and indeed with regard to those from the Classical traditions, one that conforms more easily to the standard Western ideal; although I am not for one moment implying that these images are more beautiful than any of her others. Why then are the coin portraits, which show Cleopatra with a strong masculine profile, the most commonly cited to prove her ugliness? It is almost as if it is preferable for Cleopatra not to have been of great beauty. It is also a sad indictment of the modern western stereotype of what is, and is not, attractive.

Cleopatra's beauty is often linked to the downfall of the queen and her admirers, as in Lucan's Pharsalia (line 164). Not all Roman writers were quite as shallow as their modern counterparts. Plutarch refers to the queen's inner beauty and charisma in several parts of *The Life of Antony* and in chapter 73 states that

Cleopatra was "conscious and intensely proud of her personal beauty." The denial of Cleopatra's physical beauty and so her perceived power over men, has been questioned in much the same way as Cleopatra's African heritage. Both issues are far more complicated than they seem initially. How do we (and more to the point how did the ancient Egyptians) define beauty or indeed "Black"? Both identities are transient, dependent upon culture and time (Hamer 2003: 126; Shohat 2003: 129).

2

SOURCES

2.1 MODERN BIOGRAPHIES

Many biographies of Cleopatra VII draw upon Roman texts as their main sources. Modern historians are clearly aware that such texts are politically or culturally biased, but seem to use them without further thought as if they have no alternative. In this way Cleopatra is viewed as a European monarch when in fact she was ruler of Egypt.

Traditional biographies include those of Grant (first printed in 1972) and this remains the most comprehensive account based on the historical sources. Similarly Bradford's (1971) biography is divided chronologically and to some extent thematically. More recently there have been books that consider the wider subject of Cleopatra's and Ptolemaic Egypt (Chauveau 2000, and 2002 for the English translation). In 1997 a history of Cleopatra and Egypt during her reign was published to accompany a television programme produced by Timewatch (Foss 1997). The myth of Cleopatra has been addressed in two comprehensive books by Hughes-Hallett (1990) and Hamer (1993); more recently Royster (2003) published a book on Cleopatra in modern literature and media. Scholars have now started to look at particular aspects of Cleopatra's rule – for example Kleiner (2005), entitled *Cleopatra and Rome*, but which deviates from the title to include sections on Egypt taken mainly from the British Museum exhibition catalogue of 2001. In 2003 the proceedings of a conference that was held at the British Museum to accompany the exhibition was published (Walker and Ashton) and a summary of the ideas formed the basis of a more recent, smaller publication by the same authors (2006). A useful, but not exhaustive, source book in translation was produced by Jones (2006) and will be referred to throughout the text, along with more specific translations of Roman sources. This is not an exhaustive account of the available literature in English but will give the reader some idea of the scale of publications on the subject. Few other historical figures command such interest. It is not easy to extract Cleopatra from a Roman historical context; it is easy to see why many writers fail to achieve this in their biographies. This book will not ignore the Romans and their considerable influence on the framework of Cleopatra's life, but it will attempt to consider the queen within an Egyptian context.

In addition to monographs there are also exhibition catalogues, as mentioned with regard to that organized by the British Museum and held at the Palazzo Ruspoli in Rome (2000) and the Field Museum in Chicago (2002). This was not the first time that the USA had hosted an exhibition on the subject of Cleopatra. In 1988 the Brooklyn Museum produced an exhibition entitled *Cleopatra's Egypt Age of the Ptolemies* (Bianchi ed. 1988). The catalogue included essays by leading scholars, which have become staple works on a number of aspects of Ptolemaic royal representation. The objects drew upon a much wider field than Cleopatra herself and included material from the reigns of her predecessors and also her successors.

Such alternatives to the written historical record are important because they offer a means of assessing how Cleopatra wished to be presented and do not present her as simply a character within a history of another figure. Many of these sources were presented at the 2000–2002 special exhibition *Cleopatra of Egypt: from history to myth* and are conveniently illustrated in the catalogue (Walker and Higgs eds. 2001). It is not possible or indeed appropriate to explore all possible interpretations of such material in a catalogue written primarily for the general public. The exhibition and accompanying catalogue highlighted a lack of comprehensive scholarly research on many aspects of the queen's life, in particular her presentation as an Egyptian ruler. At the time of writing the present publication the scholarly community has had time to reflect on much of the work presented in the exhibition and it is now possible to reconsider how we interpret Cleopatra VII.

Unlike many earlier biographies of the queen, the present book will focus on how we interpret the surviving evidence and consider alternative evaluations. One of the greatest problems when dealing with Ptolemaic Egypt is the cross-disciplinary nature of the subject. Scholars who are trained only in one particular aspect of Ptolemaic culture seem to have difficulty in understanding what is, and is not, an acceptable interpretation of the key features and this is particularly true of the Egyptian evidence. Such problems will be explored fully in the following chapters.

2.2 TRADITIONAL ROMAN BIOGRAPHERS AND HISTORIANS

The more traditional historical narratives offer a means of exploring how Cleopatra was seen by others and, more importantly, a means to understand more about the society in which they were written. For clarification it is necessary to consider who the ancient authors were and in what political climate they were writing. Many of these writers will be familiar names. It is, however, important to consider their own backgrounds and political allegiances in order to determine how accurate their "historical narratives" really were. Below is a selective list of authors who directly mention the queen. Excerpts from their works will be quoted throughout this publication and will be compared with the archaeological and art historical evidence for the queen's reign. When considering the Roman sources it is important to remember that although writing during the Roman Imperial period, many writers and historians were Greeks and writing in Greek. The birthplaces and cultural identities are, as far as is possible, discussed briefly below under individual authors.

Contemporary Roman writers

This group of writers is significant because it allows us to see how Cleopatra was viewed by Rome during her lifetime. Julius Caesar not only played an important part in Cleopatra's life, as father of her firstborn son and chosen heir, but also wrote about his arrival and stay in two works: *The Alexandrian War* and *The Civil Wars* (book 3). Far from being a personal account, his books are written in the third person, which would accord with the work being written by Aulus Hirtius, one of his generals. Cleopatra is mentioned within the context of the death of Roman general Pompey and the political situation in Egypt at the time of Caesar's arrival (*Civil Wars* book 3.103, 107 and 108).

In contrast to the style of Julius Caesar's historical narrative and his political allegiance, the orator and politician Marcus Tullius Cicero was a fierce critic of Cleopatra. He lived from around 106–43 BCE (Jones 2006: 85–7). Cicero's letters to Atticus reveal that the queen was the subject of gossip during her two-year stay in Rome at the villa of Julius Caesar between the years 46–44 BCE. These texts are important because they date to the period before the battle of Actium and offer an account of the queen at a time when she was seen as a potential threat to Rome from her early contact with Italy.

Cicero was also not in the end a supporter of Julius Caesar, preferring to align himself politically to the general Pompey, who clashed with Caesar in the Roman civil war. Later, Cicero supported Octavian and in the years 44 and 42 BCE tried, but failed, to convince the Senate that Mark Antony should be declared a public enemy. Ironically, Cicero's allegiance to Octavian was his downfall. He fell out of favor and was murdered on December 7th, 43 BCE, himself an enemy of the state.

Augustan Roman writers – after the death of Cleopatra

Amongst the immediately post-Actium and contemporary commentators was the poet Horace who lived from 65–8 BCE (Jones

2006: 165–9). Horace was a member of a literary circle that was patronized by Augustus. He mentions Cleopatra in his first book of *Odes* (I.37), which was published around 23 BCE, seven years after the death of the queen, and which celebrates her demise with the famous line *nunc est bibendum*, "now let us drink."

Another of the inner circle of Augustus was the poet Sextus Aurelius Propertius who was born between 54–47 BCE and died in 16 BCE. He mentions Cleopatra in his love poems (Jones 2006: 169–76). Propertius frequently referred to Cleopatra's alleged sexual deviations and debauchery, showing that this part of the myth was an early development.

Also immediately after the death of Cleopatra, the historian and geographer Strabo visited Egypt between 25 and 19 BCE and mentions Cleopatra in several sections of *Geography*. It is only in book 17.1.10 that Cleopatra is discussed in any detail; the subject is the speculation surrounding her death (Jones 2006: 7, 29–30).

Tiberian Roman writers

There were several writers during the reign of Tiberius, the successor of Augustus, who mention Cleopatra VII. Naturally they were keen to praise the father of the current emperor. Tiberius himself seems to have felt little affinity with Egyptian cults in Rome, closing the main sanctuary of Isis in Rome following a scandal there. Some dedications were made in Egypt under his name, but these projects were mostly finishing those started under his father's prolific building programme (Arnold 1999: 248–50).

Velleius Paterculus was a historian who was rarely used as a source by later ancient writers. He lived from around 19 BCE until after 30 CE, when his work was published; he was a supporter of Tiberius and his government. Cleopatra, who features in book 2 of a work entitled *Histories*, is used to illustrate Mark Antony's weak character, although Mark Antony's actions are questioned and criticized independently of the queen in the sections immediately preceding that on the battle of Actium (Jones 2006: 153–4, 164–5, and 189).

Valerius Maximus was also a Tiberian historian and writer of *A collection of memorable deeds and words*. In book 4, 1:15 there is a reference to Cleopatra. With Cicero amongst his influences and the entire work aimed at flattering Tiberius it is of little surprise to find that Valerius was not a supporter of the queen.

Lucan lived from around 39–65 CE and wrote an epic poem entitled *Pharsalia* (10.1–192 and 332–546) in which the war between Caesar and Pompey was recounted, ending with Pompey's occupation of the island of Pharos in Alexandria. Soon after Caesar's arrival Pompey was murdered at the order of Ptolemy XIII, the brother of Cleopatra. Cleopatra was shown as a manipulative character, who is referred to directly in a number of verses (Jones 2006: 63–78).

The first- and second-century-CE Roman writers

Pliny (the Elder, 23–79 CE) also mentions Cleopatra in *Natural Histories* book 9 chapter 58 (Jones 2006: 106–9). His reference gives an impression of the Roman perception of the wealth and luxury of the Ptolemaic court and recounted the well-known story of Cleopatra dissolving a pearl in wine.

Cleopatra VII was not only an enemy of Rome. Flavius Josephus, who was born around 37/8 CE and died in around 100 CE, was a Jewish priest and historian who included Cleopatra amongst those who were anti-Semitic in a work entitled *Against Apion*, a second called *Jewish War* and finally *Jewish Antiquities*. Many of his historical facts are one-sided; in one particular instance he accuses the queen of "destroying the gods of her country and the sepulchres of her predecessors."

Plutarch, a major source on the last years of Cleopatra's rule, was born before 50 CE and died sometime before 125 CE (Pelling 1988: 3). He traveled to Egypt and for the last 30 years of his life was a priest at Delphi. It is often said that he was a great supporter of the relationship between Greece and Rome and as such shared the emperor Hadrian's own attitudes (Pelling 1988: 9). Cleopatra appears twice in his biographies of *Caesar* (Jones 2006: 55–8) and *Antony* (Jones 2006: see 343). It was Plutarch's *Life of Antony* that provided the basis for many later writers on Cleopatra. The queen appears as a chapter of Antony's life rather than enjoying her own history.

Also working under the emperor Hadrian, Suetonius was born in around 69 CE and was a professional scholar. He was dismissed as court writer by Hadrian in 120/1 CE. As a writer he recorded events and made simple statements rather than critical analyses of his sources. He mentions Cleopatra in three of his biographies, *Julius Caesar* (chapters 35 and 52; Jones 2006: 46–52, 54–5, 78–9, 87–8), *Augustus* (chapters 17 and 69; Jones 2006: 129–34, 144–6, 201–2), and *Nero* (chapter 3).

Galen lived from around 130–200 CE. He was a Pergamene physician who studied in Alexandria and recorded Cleopatra's cure for hair-loss (Rowlandson 1998: 41). It is possible that this was connected to Julius Caesar's baldness or perhaps a continued narrative tradition of Alexandrian scholarship and learning.

Second- and third-century-CE Roman writers

Dio lived from around 150–235 CE and was a member of the Roman Senate under the emperor Commodus. His *Roman History* includes an account of the war between Pompey and Julius Caesar and Octavian's conquest, which led to the establishment of the Roman Empire. Cleopatra is mentioned in several parts (Jones 2006: 31 and see 336). As a historian Cassius used Livy as a source.

Philostratus, a Roman citizen, lived as a child on the Athenian territory of the island of Lemnos; it is thought that he was born around 170 CE. Cleopatra is cited as an example of decadence and licentiousness in his work entitled *Lives of the Sophists* (Wright 1952). His work is a good example of how Cleopatra was seen to be a bad influence on those around her. Her viper-like grip on men was used by a number of Roman writers to explain the downfall of her Roman "victims." Cleopatra is mentioned in an example of a couplet in book 1 chapter 5 where she is discussed with regard to an Egyptian named Philostratus, who studied philosophy with the queen, in order to explain his adoption of the panegyric.

2.3 EGYPTIANS AND AFRICANS

The writers discussed so far have had no personal bond or link with Egypt beyond traveling there, and so it is of little surprise that many adopt a hostile view of Cleopatra. This section considers a number of historians who came from North Africa in order to explore the possibility that there existed a view that was contrary to that of many Roman authors. The majority, as will be seen, were Roman citizens.

Appian was born in Alexandria, probably during the reign of Domitian (Jones 2006: 38–41, 79–80, 103). He held office in the city but moved to Rome after obtaining Roman citizenship. When the narratives of Dio and Appian are compared, the difference in attitudes of the two writers is quite apparent (Gowing 1992). Although Appian shared the established idea that Cleopatra and Alexandria were a negative influence upon an already weak Antony, he does not blame her Egyptian background, nor does he describe the Egyptians as the troublesome characters that appear in many examples of Roman literature (Gowing 1992: 115, 117–18). It has also been suggested that Appian, as an Egyptian, did not necessarily consider the Roman conquest to have been an improvement to the government of Egypt (Gowing 1992: 115 n.60). It seems likely that it did not suit an Alexandrian historian to admit that his city had directly contributed to Antony's downfall (Gowing 1992: 122).

Also from Egypt, Athenaeus wrote a work entitled the *Learned Banqueters* some time after the death of Commodus in 192 CE. Born in the Egyptian Delta town of Naukratis, as a writer he is better known for his wit than for his historical accuracy. Nevertheless, his work has become an important source for Ptolemaic festivals and his mention of Cleopatra in book 4 refers to the luxury of her banquets (Thompson 2000).

The late first to second century African-born historian and poet Florus seems to have felt no affinity with the queen. The sources for his Roman history were Livy, Sallust, Caesar, Seneca the Elder, Virgil, and Lucan (Jones 2006: 62), and, although African by birth, Florus lived in Rome with a short period in Spain, returning to Italy during the reign of the emperor Hadrian. The idea that Cleopatra was a prostitute, and *femme fatale*, was also shared by the fourth-century-CE African governor and writer Aurelius Victor, in his Republican biographies *On Famous Men*.

2.4 EARLY CHRISTIAN AND MOSLEM EGYPTIAN HISTORIANS

There was perhaps an Egyptian narrative alternative to the written Roman history, which was not recorded until the seventh century CE, when John, Bishop of Nikiou in Upper Egypt wrote a *Chronicle* (El Daly 2004: 132). It has recently been suggested that the book was written in Arabic rather than Greek or Coptic (el-Daly 2004: 132 quoting Abd Al-Galil 2000: 260–2). In his *Chronicle* John wrote that Cleopatra was "the most illustrious and wise among women" (translation by Charles 1916: 48–50). This concept was repeated by tenth-century Moslem writers, such as Al-Masudi who described Cleopatra as "the last of the wise ones of Greece" (El Daly 2004: 133).

The Cleopatra who appears in early Moslem texts was a wholly different character to her portrayal by Roman writers and historians (El Daly 2004: 121–2; 130–7; 142). She was shown as a scholar, physician, scientist, philosopher, and builder (albeit confused by being associated with building projects undertaken by her predecessors). The *Arab Romance of Cleopatra* (El Daly 2004: 135–6) finds the queen assimilated to Alexander, which is testimony to her status as a historical figure. As El Daly notes the Cleopatra of the *Romance* is an intelligent woman with great political ambition, a woman who also appears in some of the

Roman sources, such as the final chapters of Plutarch's *Life of Antony*. It is possible that the Arab writers and Moslem historians used some of the same sources as utilized by the traditional Roman writers; they simply chose to enhance a more favorable side of the queen's personality and to celebrate her political aspirations and strength. It is highly ironic, given the widely peddled western perception of modern Islamic culture, that it is within the Islamic tradition that we find Cleopatra treated as any male historical figure. Those who are more familiar with the perception of Cleopatra in modern Egypt, however, would not be surprised to find a favorable history of the queen firmly embedded within earlier Islamic cultural traditions.

2.5 ALTERNATIVES TO THE LITERARY AND HISTORICAL SOURCES

Substitutes for the Roman historical accounts exist. These alternative sources range from images of the queen (statues, coinage, temple reliefs), and the temples themselves, and include decrees issued during her reign. Such evidence still requires analysis and so there is still scope for misinterpretation, but these are particularly important when considering Cleopatra as an Egyptian. These sources may not lend themselves as well to historical narrative or make reference to the character of the queen, but they constitute a primary rather than secondary source of information and are potentially less biased than written accounts because they do not represent another's opinion.

There are a number of examples of Egyptian textual evidence relating to the reign of Cleopatra VII, ranging from documented cult titles, affiliation to established divinities and, in terms of administration, royal decrees and papyri. One of the most controversial papyrus fragments is the so-called Cleopatra papyrus; a royal document controversially believed by some to show a signature in the queen's own hand, reading: "let it happen," but with a typo in the ancient Greek (van Minnen 2003). Irrespective of the author's identity, such documents present important political evidence for Cleopatra's rule and will be discussed fully later in this book.

Stelae and temples offer further evidence for Cleopatra's Egypt. The queen's dedications at Edfu, Armant, Koptos, and Denderah, all of which are in Upper Egypt, and in Alexandria at the temples of Isis and Caesar allow the modern historian to study patterns of patronage and also show with whom the queen wished to be associated, both in terms of her consort and the gods. The relief decorations and statues from these sites also illustrate how Cleopatra was presented, as both queen and goddess. A Greek equivalent can be found in the form of coins that were minted in Alexandria and in Ptolemaic overseas possessions. Outside Egypt and the Ptolemaic Empire, in Rome there are statues and sanctuaries that can be linked to the queen's two-year stay in the city in addition of course to the aforementioned literary sources.

3

KING'S DAUGHTER, KING'S SISTER, GREAT ROYAL WIFE

3.1 POLITICS AND THE IDEOLOGY OF KINGSHIP

Cleopatra VII should be considered as a globally aware and politically astute leader. In order to understand her role within a wider context it is necessary to take into account a wider historical framework. This introductory section is not intended as a full historical overview of the Ptolemaic period up to the reign of Cleopatra VII; for this Günther Hölbl's *History of the Ptolemaic Empire* provides an up-to-date overview of key themes (2001). This section will rather introduce the reader to some of the key aspects relevant to Ptolemaic culture and go some way to explaining the background of the domestic policies of Cleopatra VII. References by Roman writers and historians to the Ptolemaic royal family are, like those to Cleopatra VII, generally unfavorable. Documentary evidence in the form of decrees, letters, and ostraka (re-used pot sherds and fragments of stone) from within Egypt is of considerably more help in determining trends within the fluctuating power and fortunes of the Ptolemaic dynasty. Like the building programmes, these sources often reveal a lack of willingness to admit defeat on behalf of the rulers.

The ideology of Ptolemaic kingship has largely been interpreted from a Greek perspective, rather than linking the new administration to the previous and existing government of Egypt at the time of Macedonian succession. The Egyptians were dependent upon the notion of an appointed ruling king in order for their ideological universe to function. That the physical presence in Egypt of a king on the Egyptian throne was not crucial to the survival of Egypt as a state is illustrated by the absent rule of the Persians and then Alexander and his immediate successors, all of whom employed representatives in their absence. The Romans employed similar tactics following the death of Cleopatra VII. Egypt needed a resident king to discourage invasion from a foreign foe, in the case of the Ptolemies another Macedonian ruler, or later the Romans. Egyptians had, on a small but significant number of occasions, accepted a woman as ruler, and royal women often played a crucial role in both religion and politics. Macedonia, from where Alexander and Ptolemy I came, produced powerful royal women, unlike Classical Greece (Pomeroy 1990: 3–11; Ashton 2003a: 13–15).

There were two strands to domestic Egyptian kingship: firstly the administration/government of the country, and secondly their religious role and place within the cosmos. Underlying these two traditional objectives was the predicament in which foreign rulers of Egypt found themselves – the acculturation of their own traditions with those of their new country. That the Ptolemies were at the heart of the structure of the administration of Egypt has always been a core part of modern historical interpretation of their rule (Delia 1993: 192–5). In 1993 Samuel argued that, although the ideology of Ptolemaic kingship was closely linked to the administration of Egypt, the organization was not as tightly controlled as has sometimes been thought. The idea that the Ptolemies changed the way in which Egypt was run only as was necessary (Samuel 1993: 175), in an ad hoc manner, seems to me to be a logical one. Papyri show how the rulers encouraged their Greek settlers, mainly soldiers, in areas such as the Fayoum by awarding them pieces of land (Hölbl 2001: 61–2). Others, officials who were close to the early rulers, were awarded estates. This was an extension of the *Philoi* (literally "friends") system of governing. *Philoi* were close advisors of the king and as a system derived from Macedonian royal court. The successors of Alexander had themselves performed a similar role. Such advisors were found in their greatest number during the reigns of the first two Ptolemies; their role dwindled during the reign of Ptolemy

III (Samuel 1993: 185–6). During the troubled reigns of the boy kings, Ptolemies V and VI, court politicians became a threat to the royal house by attempting to manipulate the young rulers (Samuel 1993:187–8).

Royal decrees clearly illustrate the fortunes of the Ptolemaic dynasty. A comparison between the trilingual Canopus decree of Ptolemy III and the better known Rosetta decree has become a standard essay question for students of Ptolemaic Egypt. The Canopus decree of 238 BCE honors the ruling household and illustrates the importance of religion, cult, and political power (Hölbl 2001: 105–11). The second section of the decree concentrates on the burial rites of a daughter of Ptolemy III, who had recently died whilst still a child. Both sections of the decree illustrate how the priests advised upon and developed royal iconography and ideology; details of the costume assigned to the new goddess Berenice are meticulously recorded. Copies of this decree were placed in all major temples throughout Egypt.

The reign of Ptolemy IV Philopator is generally seen as a major turning point for the dynasty. The Raphia decree was written following Philopator's victory against the Syrian king on June 22, 217 BCE (Hölbl 2001: 162–4). Like the Rosetta and Canopus decrees the Raphia decree was trilingual. The king appears Greek-style on horseback with a spear, wearing the Egyptian crowns of Upper and Lower Egypt. Behind him is his sister and wife Arsinoe III, with the usual royal headdress. Such images of the king in battle were especially common on the temple reliefs of Ramesses II (at Karnak and Luxor temples) and Ramesses III (on his funerary temple at Medinat Habu on the West Bank at Thebes). On the Raphia stela a scaled-down version is shown; however, the message is still the same. Here, Ptolemy IV enacts his role as defender of Egypt. The iconography alone presents a strong ideological and political message (Hölbl 2001: 165).

The Rosetta decree dates to 196 BCE and paints a very different picture to its earlier counterparts (Hölbl 2001: 165–6). The same careful attention to detail is still present when describing the cult statues of Ptolemy V that were to be placed in every

Egyptian temple. The priests who were to administer the new royal cult of their teenage king bestowed honors upon themselves (Hölbl 2001: 165). Perhaps most telling of the troubled times is the reduction in taxes and amnesty on certain crimes that were awarded to the general population of Egypt. These amnesties were awarded in light of contemporary rebellions and uprisings in Egypt. As Hölbl concludes in his discussion of the decree, it shows a king who enacts his ritual role but one who is forced to submit to the wishes of the priests (2001: 166).

Throughout the Ptolemaic period trends can be seen to emerge: the golden age of Ptolemaic rule being the reigns of the first three kings. The reign of Ptolemy IV has always been seen as a point of change, a transformation during which the king lost control of Egypt and the court – mostly, if the ancient writer Athenaeus is to be believed, on account of his licentious behavior (Deipnosophistai 12.549e). Similarly, the troubled reigns of Ptolemies V and VI, both young when they came to power, are seen as instrumental in the downfall of the dynasty.

Following the death of Ptolemy V his wife, Cleopatra I, ruled with their son, Ptolemy VI; her daughter, who would become Cleopatra II, remained in the Ptolemaic court. The situation that Cleopatra II found herself in, following the death of her mother Cleopatra I in 176 BCE, was similar in many respects to that of Cleopatra VII. She had two brothers and was married to the elder, Ptolemy VI, in 176 BCE probably in an attempt to stabilize family relationships (Whitehorne 1994: 89). Six years later Ptolemy VIII, the younger brother, joined his siblings on the throne of Egypt (Whitehorne 1994: 93 for discussion). Ptolemy VI was then removed from power and Ptolemy VIII and Cleopatra II were set up as rulers (Hölbl 2001: 183–6). According to Livy (45.11.6) it was Cleopatra who brought about peace and the three attempted to rule together once more. The problems continued; however, being a woman had its benefits and Cleopatra II was the constant member of any alliance, her unenviable role in fact allowing her more flexibility and power than either of her brothers.

Following the death of Ptolemy VI, in 145 BCE, Ptolemy VIII married his sister and murdered his nephew Ptolemy VII, it is said by Justin on their wedding day, thus removing the rightful heir to the throne. The troubled sole reign of Ptolemy VIII, partially caused by the strength of Cleopatras II and III, with whom he ruled together, is often cited as a point of no return for the dynasty's fortunes. During this time Rome was asked to intervene on behalf of Ptolemy VIII. In return, and as an insurance, he promised his kingdom to Rome in the event of his death without an heir (Hölbl 2001: 187).

In 132/1 BCE Cleopatra II organized a revolt against her consort and brother Ptolemy VIII, who was exiled to Cyprus with his second wife and niece Cleopatra III. Diodorus (34–5.14) and Justin (38.12–13) record his response: he murdered their son, Memphites, and sent the body to his sister. Cleopatra II continued to rule with Ptolemy VIII. In spite of this third atrocity – the first two being the murder of Ptolemy VII and the rape of Cleopatra III – in 130 BCE a second triple rule of Ptolemy VIII, Cleopatra II (the sister), and Cleopatra III (the wife) followed, and was equally fraught as the earlier alliance but lasted until 116 BCE.

Late in the reign of Ptolemy VIII, Cleopatra II, and Cleopatra III an amnesty was declared on all crimes except murder and sacrilege (P. Tebt. 5). At the same time Ptolemy VIII was funding one of the most expansive temple building programmes of the dynasty throughout Egypt at traditional Egyptian religious centres (Ashton 2003b: 217–19). Under Ptolemy VIII the Egyptian aristocracy and common population alike were considered in an attempt to settle the political situation following the civil wars. New cities were founded in the south of Egypt during the reigns of Ptolemies VI or VIII. The troops settled here in the same way that the early Greek settlers had settled in the Fayoum during the reigns of Ptolemies I and II. Such policies were a weakened extension of those under the first rulers of the dynasty, when Greeks were rewarded with land (Thompson 2006: 98–104; Rowlandson 2003: 254–9).

In 116 BCE Ptolemy VIII left Egypt to his preferred wife, Cleopatra III (Justin 39.3.1), although her mother was still alive and ruled with her daughter for the first year following their husband's death. This placed the younger queen in a strong and yet vulnerable position. According to the will of Ptolemy VIII she was permitted to choose with which of her sons she would rule. In reality, she was forced to alternate her allegiance between the two, depending initially on her mother's choice and then with which of the sons was most popular with the Alexandrians (Hölbl 2001: 205). Cleopatra III is generally painted in a sympathetic light, in her early years as a victim of her uncle Ptolemy VIII's lust, which as noted resulted in the unhappy joint rule of the ruler, Cleopatra II and her daughter Cleopatra III (Justin 38.8). Behind these later literary impressions was a woman who clearly aimed to advance her power and status. Her son Ptolemy X clearly saw her as a threat and in 101 BCE she was murdered.

3.2 THE PRESENTATION OF PTOLEMAIC KINGSHIP

The divisions between Hellenistic Greek and Egyptian kingship are not always immediately apparent and are colored by the way in which modern scholarship approaches the subject. Egyptologists easily find parallels from earlier periods, whereas Classical scholars are quick to compare the developments in other Hellenistic kingdoms, sometimes unaware that these parallels are firmly routed in other native traditions.

The ideology of kingship can be traced through the aforementioned decrees. The archaeological record can also elucidate whether the rulers saw themselves as Greek or Egyptian kings and reveals an interesting shift in portrayal of the royal house at the start of the second century BCE. Early rulers, Ptolemies I–IV, copied the features of the Egyptian-style statues of the rulers of Thirtieth Dynasty. This traditional style continued until the end of the Ptolemaic period (Ashton 2003b: 218–20; 2004b: 545). but during the reign of Ptolemy V a new phenomenon emerged (Ashton 2001a: 25–36; Stanwick 2002: 56–7 and 85–8). The Egyptian artists start to produce sculptures that display the Greek portrait type of the male rulers, and some show hair beneath the headdresses. The representations of royal women mimic those of their consorts. At the same time Greek-style "portraits" were produced by and on behalf of the early rulers. These images are largely identified by comparing sculpture with the images of rulers and their queens on coins. Some show the non-idealized forms of rulers such as Ptolemy VIII and his sons Ptolemies IX and X. During this time there is a decrease in the numbers of Greek-style statues. The coins minted during the reigns of Ptolemies IX and X also cease to use the royal portrait on the obverse. This feature was reintroduced during the reign of Ptolemy XII, Cleopatra's father.

In contrast the presentation of the consorts of rulers on the walls of Egyptian temples forms a catalogue of the escalation of the ritual and political power of Ptolemaic queens. They also offer a directory of allegiances, but show how the rulers wanted to be seen rather than the reality. This is particularly true of the reign of Ptolemy VIII, who usually appears with his two wives even though he and Cleopatra III spent some time in exile. The unified triad that appears on numerous walls was not entirely the reality. As a source the temple reliefs remain largely untapped; nevertheless they are particularly important with regard to the presentation of the power of Ptolemaic royal women.

3.3 CLEOPATRA: KING'S DAUGHTER

The identity of Cleopatra's paternal grandmother is unknown. Her grandfather, Ptolemy IX, was married to two of his sisters: Cleopatra IV and Cleopatra Selene, but the mother of Ptolemy XII was a concubine.

The traditional family tree shows three children from this branch: Ptolemy XII, Ptolemy of Cyprus and Cleopatra V (Tryphaina). According to the traditional Ptolemaic family tree Ptolemy XII married his sister and they produced Cleopatra Berenice IV, Cleopatra VI (Tryphaina), Cleopatra VII, Arsinoe, Ptolemy XIII, and Ptolemy XIV (Walker and Higgs 2001 and Whitehorne 1994: 174–87).

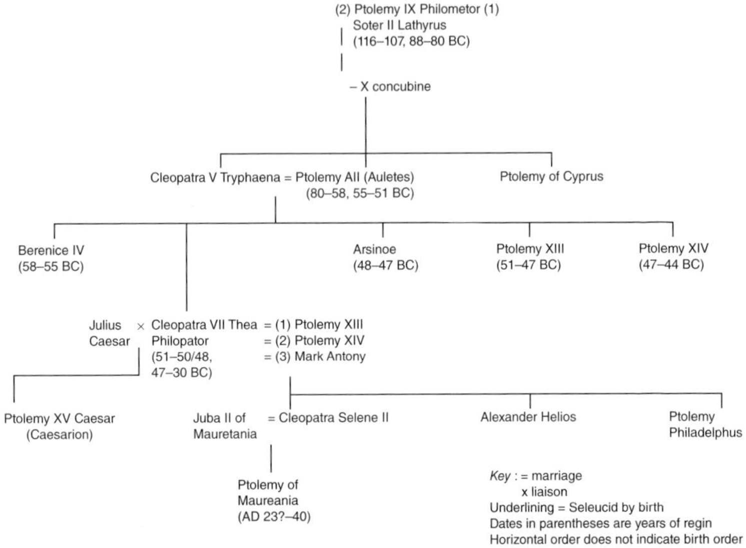

Figure 3.1 The Ptolemies from Ptolemy V and Cleopatra I

However, in 2001 Hölbl devised an alternative tree in which Cleopatra Selene, wife of Ptolemy IX, is allocated the title of Cleopatra V, Cleopatra Tryphaina the sister of Ptolemy XII becoming Cleopatra VI Tryphaina. According to this tree the only child from the union of Ptolemy XII and Cleopatra VI Tryphaina was Cleopatra Berenice IV (2001: 223). The other children, including Cleopatra VII, were born to an unknown mother, which makes not only Ptolemy XII illegitimate, but also four of his children. It has been suggested that the mother of Cleopatra VII, Arsinoe, and the two Ptolemies was an Egyptian, perhaps even a member of a priestly family from Memphis (Huß 1990). Cleopatra Tryphaina was removed from the dating formulae in 69 BCE, which supports the idea that she was not the mother of all of Ptolemy XII's children (Hölbl 2001: 223).

Ptolemy XII came to the throne following the murder of Ptolemy XI, as the Alexandrians' choice (Hölbl 2001: 222); his other brother became Ptolemy of Cyprus. Following the usual

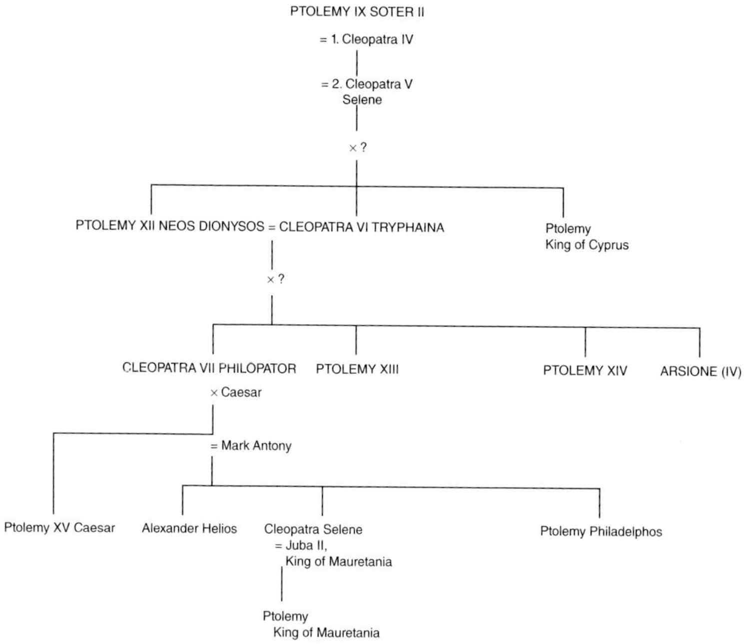

Figure 3.2 Ptolemaic family from Ptolemy V to the end of their history

Ptolemaic tradition Ptolemy XII married his sister Cleopatra Tryphaina and their first child was named Cleopatra Berenice IV. Ptolemy XII adopted the titles Father-loving god (*Theos Philopator*) and Sibling-loving (*Philadelphos*), the first stressing his right as the illegitimate son of Ptolemy IX to rule and the second perhaps as a means of looking back to the dynasty's golden age (Hölbl 2001: 223), a strategy that would be copied by Cleopatra VII (Ashton 2003a: 93–5). Ptolemy XII also took the cult title of New Dionysos (*Neos Dionysos*), and was awarded the nickname Auletes due to his accomplished playing of the flute (Strabo 17.1.11; Athenodorus 5.206d). A marble Greek-style statue representing Ptolemy XII (Walker and Higgs 2001: 157, no. 155) shows the ruler with the mitra (headband across the forehead) of

Dionysos, indicating a link between sculptural representation and the titles held by the King. The statue appears to have been recut from an earlier representation of a ruler with a fuller face, most likely one of the Physcons, Ptolemy VIII, or Ptolemy IX his son and the father of Ptolemy XII.

Ptolemy XII was heavily dependent upon the Romans, and as their "friendship" put an increased strain upon the Egyptian economy, his rule came under increasing scrutiny from the Egyptian elite. In around 58 BCE, 18 years after he had come to power, Ptolemy XII was exiled and Cleopatra Tryphaina became the official ruler of Egypt. Some scholars believe that this Cleopatra was in fact a different woman to the sister and wife of Ptolemy XII and that her name had been removed from the dating formula ten years earlier because she had died, rather than falling out of favor (Whitehorne 1994: 178, 182–3). It seems plausible that a wife could fall out of favor only to reappear taking control of Egypt some years later; there are after all a number of precedents in the years immediately before Ptolemy XII's reign, perhaps most notably Cleopatra III, his grandmother. More immediately, documents indicate that Cleopatra Tryphaina ruled with her daughter Cleopatra Berenice IV but died towards the end of 57 BCE, a year after coming to power (Hölbl 2001: 227). In 55 BCE, with the support of the Romans, Ptolemy XII was back on the throne and started his second reign. Cleopatra Berenice, who, it is to be remembered, was his first born, and her supporters were put to death. In 52 BCE Ptolemy XII took his 17-year-old daughter Cleopatra (VII) as his co-ruler. The children were all awarded the cult title of the New Sibling-loving Gods (*Theoi Neoi Philadelphoi*). By accepting rule with her father rather than conspiring to work against him, Cleopatra VII showed herself to be politically astute.

Ptolemy XII was a prolific builder, a characteristic that ironically seems often to reveal a weak or threatened ruler. In Upper Egypt a gateway was added to the Ptah temple at Karnak (Plate 3.1). This small temple had received previous gateways from earlier rulers since its foundation. Its importance is probably due to its position – it is just south of the main temple enclosure

Plate 3.1 The Ptah temple, Karnak

wall, which dates to Thirtieth Dynasty or the early Ptolemaic period. The Ptah temple is placed on the main northwest *dromos* leading from the main temple of Amun, past a series of chapels and towards the gateway that led through to the Montu enclosure. The gateway is small and would not have cost a great deal of money to build. Many of the cartouches were left blank. The temple of Horus and Sobek at Kom Ombo was also substantially enlarged under Ptolemy XII, leaving the early temple of Ptolemies VI and VIII intact. As with many of his other projects the focus of the building was on the front of the temple, where a substantial *pronaos* was built (Plate 3.2). It has also been suggested that the stone enclosure wall dates to the reign of Ptolemy XII (Arnold 1999: 220). In the Delta a limestone addition to the sanctuary of Triphis at Athribis was built, including a *pronaos* and hypostyle hall and chambers (Arnold 1999: 211–12).

Ptolemy XII also appears on the relief decoration of the crypts at Armant (Hermonthis). He appears alone (Plate 3.3) in the first crypt wearing a blue crown, making an offering to a

Plate 3.2 The temple *pronaos* at Kom Ombo, reign of Ptolemy XII

Plate 3.3 Ptolemy XII wearing a blue crown from the crypts at Armant

Plate 3.4 The Buchis bull from the crypts at Armant

hawk-headed god representing Montu Re-Harakhty, Isis, and Horus (Thiers and Volokhine 2005: 10, 29–32, figs. 16–17). The names are in the same form as those at Kom Ombo. In other parts of the same crypt the more generic Pr-aa (Pharaoh) appears (Plate 3.4), and is accompanied by a relief showing the Buchis bull. In the second crypt Ptolemy XII appears with the same titles (Thiers and Volokhine 2005: 38–41). On the east wall of the second crypt Ptolemy XII wears the crown of Upper Egypt (Plate 3.5; Thiers and Volokhine 2005: 60 fig. 53).

In addition to his coronation Ptolemy XII visited Memphis on at least one other occasion (Thompson 1988: 139). The close bond between Ptolemy XII and the priesthood at Memphis is illustrated by a stela (dedicatory relief) now in the British Museum (Andrews in Walker and Higgs 2001: 184–6, no. 192). The deceased High Priest Pasherenptah III appears at the top of the stela in front of an offering table and before the Egyptian gods Osiris, Ptah, Isis, Nephthys, Horus, Anubis, Imhotep, and a standard. The text offers an autobiography of the priest's life and

Plate 3.5 Ptolemy XII wearing the crown of Upper Egypt from the crypts at Armant

states that he performed the coronation of Ptolemy XII in 76 BCE. In return, when the priest visited Alexandria by chariot he was honored with the title of Priest of the Royal Cult and given a gold chaplet. Pasherenptah died during the reign of Cleopatra VII on July 14, 41 BCE.

In the far south of Egypt, Ptolemy XII further developed the temple of Isis at Philae, and decorated the first pylon. A naos (shrine) of Ptolemy XII was also found at Dabod, which is just south of Aswan (Arnold 1999: 221). It is clear, however, that the key area of development during his reign was Upper Egypt and the temples that have formed the core of the modern tourist Nile cruise.

Coins minted during the reign of Ptolemy XII bore his image, but not that of his consort. A youthful, godlike figure with strong chin and aquiline nose can be found on the obverse of his Alexandrian coins, a portrait type that would later be adopted by Cleopatra and Mark Antony. There is only one possible image of Ptolemy XII and Cleopatra VII during their co-rule – and it is important to stress that the female may well represent Cleopatra Tryphaina – a clay papyrus seal from Edfu and now housed in the Royal Ontario Museum (Ashton 2001b: 158, no. 157). The sealing (Plate 3.6) shows a youthful male figure, with unkempt hair, styled in a manner similar to that of Ptolemy XII's coins. The female is positioned jugate behind the male; she has a prominent nose and appears to wear a crown (*stephane*) rather than the royal diadem indicating that she is a goddess and not simply a ruler. Although it has been suggested (Kyrieleis 1975: pl. 68.5) that this pair is Ptolemy XII and his sister, I see no iconographic reason why the female could not represent his daughter Cleopatra VII.

The Egyptian names taken by Ptolemy XII influenced those of his male successors, so much so that there is a great deal of confusion in identifying the names of Ptolemies XII, XIII, XIV, and XV (Traunecker 1992: 272–3). Of the Greek titles, Cleopatra herself adopted Father-loving, and Sibling-loving (*Philadelphos*) was the name chosen for her fourth child Ptolemy. Just as Ptolemy XII was New Dionysos, so the queen became New Isis. Thus Cleopatra was not only influenced by the policies of her father but seems to have continued his cult affiliations. In documentary evidence Ptolemy XII started by calling himself Theos Philopator and Philadelphos; the title of Neos Dionysos was then slipped into the formula so that a typical document

Plate 3.6 Clay seal impression showing a representation of Ptolemy XII and Cleopatra V or VII. With permission of the Royal Ontario Museum © ROM

would read "King Ptolemy, God, New Dionysos, Father-loving, Sibling-loving" (Gauthier 1916: 397). A later stela used the following formulae: "On behalf of King Ptolemy, God New Dionysos and his children the Gods New Sibling-loving" (Gauthier 1916: 400). Cleopatra VII's adoption of the title Father-loving served two purposes. Firstly it continued the title used by her own father and secondly it linked her to him as his rightful heir.

Ptolemy XII was dependent upon Rome for his power and position as ruler of Egypt. Cleopatra inherited this debt and soon found herself relying on Rome in order to quash a substantial rebellion by the Alexandrians. Unlike any of her predecessors Cleopatra turned this potentially weak situation around to her own benefit. She did so by having children with two influential Roman generals. If the historical sources are to be believed, Cleopatra brought about the downfall of the Romans with whom she was directly involved.

3.4 LITERARY SOURCES: FAMILY POLITICS

Several Roman written sources discuss the relationship between Ptolemy XII's children and there are references to the queen's joint rule with her brothers within the archaeological and papyrological evidence. Lucan refers to Cleopatra's sibling marriages in lines 110–113 and 430–455 of his epic *Pharsalia*; in the first instance regarding the transfer of power from the king (Ptolemy XIII) to his sister on account of her relationship with Caesar and, secondly, as a means of perverse comparison to the killing of Pompey.

Strabo mentions Cleopatra's direct family in book 17 (1.11): the banishment of Auletes (Cleopatra's father), his three daughters, and two sons, and the eldest sister's rule with an unsuitable husband; we are told that Cleopatra's sister strangled him on account of his vulgarity. In Suetonius' *Deified Julius Caesar* the reader is told that Caesar handed over Egypt to Cleopatra and her younger brother for fear that, if it were to become a province, a governor might incite revolution there (35).

Josephus takes advantage of an opportunity, in discussing Antony's gift of Coele Syria to the queen, to slight Cleopatra's character by exploring her family affairs (*Jewish Antiquities* 15 4.1.88–95): "Since she was prone to covetousness by nature, there was no lawless deed which she did not commit; she had already caused the death by poisoning her brother when he was only 15 years old because she knew that he was to become king, and she had her sister Arsinoe killed by Antony when she was a suppliant at the temple of Artemis in Ephesus" (see also

Cassius Dio 48.24.2). Josephus again refers to the murder of Cleopatra's brother and sister in *Against Apion* (book 2.5).

3.5 CLEOPATRA AND HER BROTHERS

In 51 BCE Ptolemy XII died, leaving Egypt to Cleopatra VII and his elder son Ptolemy XIII. Recently it has been suggested that Cleopatra might have ruled alone for the first year after her father's death (Bingen 2007: 68). It is thought that no formal marriage ceremony between Ptolemy XIII and his sister took place, and that the two simply ruled together (Hölbl 2001: 231). The rule between the ten-year-old brother and sister was fraught with problems from the start. Supporters of the king had gained control of the throne by 50 BCE (Hölbl 2001: 231–9), and Cleopatra's name appeared after that of her brother, indicating that he was the dominant ruler. By 49 BCE two dating systems were running: year 1 of Ptolemy XIII's reign, which was year 3 of the joint rule. The order in which the dates were listed indicates that year 1 of the new reign was the most important. Around this time Ptolemy XIII had three new guardians: Potheinos, Achillas, and one of his teachers, Theodotos of Chios. This group contrived to oust Cleopatra from the throne and by 49 BCE achieved their aim (Hölbl 2001: 232). By the autumn of 49 BCE the Romans declared Ptolemy XIII sole ruler of Egypt. Julius Caesar described this period in his own words as part of his histories. In the *Alexandrian War* (33) Caesar states that he appointed the two siblings Ptolemy and Cleopatra as rulers, as designated in the will of Ptolemy XII. Arsinoe, Cleopatra's sister, was banished and legions were left to "support the power of King's because of their loyalty to Caesar." In Caesar's *Civil Wars*, there is a commentary on the situation in Ptolemaic Egypt immediately before the arrival of the Romans in Alexandria. Within the context of Pompey's death Caesar wrote: "As it happened, King Ptolemy was there, a mere boy, who was waging war with large forces against his sister Cleopatra. A few months ago, by means of his intimates and favourites he had expelled her from his kingdom. Cleopatra's camp was not far away from his" (3.103).

Once in Alexandria Caesar wrote: "Meanwhile thinking that the quarrels of the royal family concerned both the Roman people and himself as consul, and that he had all the more duty to act because it was in his earlier consulship that an alliance had been formed with Ptolemy, the present king's father, by a law and decree of the Senate, he announced that he had decided that king Ptolemy and his sister Cleopatra should dismiss the armies they had and settle their quarrels by submitting them to him for judgement rather than by force of arms between themselves . . ." (3.107).

Book 3.108 of the *Civil Wars* is similar in its references to Cleopatra in the *Alexandrian War*, discussing the will of Ptolemy XII in which the elder of the two sons and elder of the two daughters are named as heirs and that Rome supervised this, having been asked to see this implemented. The implication is that Caesar was involved out of duty.

3.6 THE SIBLING GODS

The eldest, possibly half, sister of Cleopatra met her death following the return of Ptolemy XII from exile. Cleopatra clearly learnt an important lesson and, as we have seen, associated herself with her father rather than working to conspire against him. Arsinoe, whose date of birth is not known, was clearly not so astute in determining the boundaries of power. During the civil war Arsinoe escaped from the palaces with her tutor Ganymedes and joined the troops led by the advisor to Ptolemy XIII, Achillas, and she was declared queen (Dio Cassius 42.39.1). Quarrels ensued and Ganymedes seized power from Achillas and the other advisor Potheinos; both were put to death by Julius Caesar, leaving Ganymedes as the main protagonist. By the end of this particular chapter Ptolemy XIII was dead and Cleopatra was back in charge of the throne but with her younger brother Ptolemy XIV at her side (Bingen 2007: 71). Arsinoe was exiled to Ephesus in Turkey. According to Josephus (*Jewish Antiquities* 15 4.1.89), Arsinoe, who had ruled Egypt briefly as Arsinoe IV, would later be put to death at the order of her sister through Mark Antony (Hölbl 2001: 236–7, 241).

3.7 INFLUENCES ON CLEOPATRA'S EARLY RULE

Cleopatra's rule was heavily influenced by the policies of her father not least of all the inherited relationship with Rome. Her joint rule with her father was a short one, but it was enough for her to secure herself a position of power and to make her a real contender for the Egyptian throne. Ptolemy XII used building projects as a means of promoting his position as ruler, particularly in the south amongst the Egyptian elite. Some of these projects were completed by his daughter, most famously Denderah, which was started four years before his death and which was not completed until the Roman period (Arnold 1999: 212–13). Another large scale building scheme was the additions to the temple of Horus at Edfu, which began early in the reign on February 2, 70 BCE (Arnold 1999: 216–20). Here, a pylon and courtyard, which functioned as a giant sundial, were built. The courtyard was closed with a monumental gateway that may have been completed during the rule of Cleopatra (Arnold 1999: 220). The pylon (Plate 3.7) was originally decorated with the Egyptian names of Cleopatra Tryphaina, but these were removed following her fall from favor (Huß 1990). The remaining images show Ptolemy XII smiting his enemies in traditional Egyptian manner before the god Horus. At Koptos Ptolemy XII built a south gate and enclosure wall, but it is generally believed that the decoration was not completed until the Roman period (Arnold 1999: 216). There are also blocks attributed to Ptolemy XII from the site (Petrie Museum UC 14523), possibly from the south gateway, which may also have been associated with the building of the Geb shrine. Cleopatra too would dedicate a Geb shrine at Koptos.

Plate 3.7 The temple of Horus, Edfu. The pylon shows an image of Ptolemy XII smiting his enemies

Cleopatra showed no interest in completing or being associated with other projects that were started by her father, and it has been suggested that the queen targeted specific deities (Ray 2001). It also seems that Cleopatra did not use her father's temples as a means of strengthening her link to him. This can be seen in the decorative programme at Denderah, where she chose to be associated with her new co-ruler and anticipated successor, Ptolemy XV. There is one possible exception to this observation – the Geb shrine at Koptos (Plate 3.8). Unlike the later temple reliefs at Denderah, where Cleopatra stands behind her son Ptolemy XV, or promotes him as the sole cult participant, on the Geb shrine the queen appears independent of her consort in individual sections of the relief rather than in a pair. The male ruler also stands alone offering in another section of the decorated interior. Cleopatra's name also appears as sole practitioner on the gateway of a temple of uncertain date from Kalabsha (Bianchi 2003: 15).

Plate 3.8 The Geb shrine, Koptos. Cleopatra stands alone offering to the gods. Petrie Museum of Egyptian Archaeology, University College London

3.8 DEDICATIONS FROM CLEOPATRA'S EARLY RULE

Koptos

Ptolemy XII's work at Koptos has already been mentioned above. As noted, Cleopatra appears on a small shrine dedicated to the god Geb (Plate 3.8). The outer walls were later decorated with the image of her successor Augustus, no doubt for political rather than religious reasons (Plate 3.9). Cleopatra stands in front of Min, Isis, and Horus (Traunecker 1992: 285) presenting a jar of incense. The queen wears the sun-disk, cow's horns, and double plume crown that was typically associated with the Ptolemaic queens. Her name appeared in two cartouches. The illustrated

Plate 3.9 The Geb shrine, Koptos. On the outside of the shrine is a representation of Augustus

relief (Plate 3.8) is accompanied by a text reading: "Woman of the two lands, Cleopatra Philopator (Father-loving), beloved of Min-Re of Koptos, king's wife, king's daughter, the great ruler . . . who reaches the height of the sky" (Traunecker 1992: 285–7; Ashton 2003d: 25–6).

There is some confusion over the identity of her consort, who, as noted, also stands alone before the gods on sections of the relief decoration on the Koptos shrine (Traunecker 1992: 322–4; Ashton 2003d: 26 n.9). It has been suggested that the male ruler represents Ptolemy XV Caesar, however the title Caesar is not present (Traunecker 1992: 322 for discussion of Weill). The cartouches are the same as those at Kom Ombo temple and are the names used by Ptolemy XII (Traunecker 1992: 272–3; Thiers and Volokline 2005: 10). Some scholars have consequently suggested that this monument was dedicated by Ptolemy XII. The use of the title "king's wife" for Cleopatra would suggest that this was not the case, unless this titulary was simply used in its symbolic and traditional sense for the king's consort irrespective of their marital status (Bianchi 2003: 18). There are earlier examples of kings taking their daughters as consorts, for example in the case of Ramesses II who took his daughters Nebettawy, Bintanat, Merytamun, and Henutmire as wives. All women took the title "great king's wife" and "king's daughter" (Grajetzki 2005: 69–70). Some (Bianchi 2003: 18) prefer to see titles such as King's sister, King's daughter, Great royal wife and in particular the title "the one who satisfies the heart of Horus" as cultic rather than literal. Bianchi concludes that the titles found at the Geb shrine are those of Ptolemy XII. It has also been suggested that the male cartouches could be associated with one of Cleopatra's brothers, on account of the shared epithets (Traunecker 1992: 320; Ashton 2003d). The problem is unlikely to be solved. Our only definite conclusion can be that the Geb shrine was an early dedication by Cleopatra VII and a male ruler, possibly Ptolemy XII or one of his sons.

If Cleopatra's status was elevated to the point that she appeared alone offering to gods during a co-rule with her father, this situation was not reflected in his will; as noted already Egypt was awarded to Cleopatra and his elder son Ptolemy XIII. However, with regard to his succession it is worth pondering the degree of influence of the Romans, who had insisted that an earlier queen should take a male consort, resulting in the disastrous and short-lived rule of Ptolemy XI. Furthermore there is nothing to suggest that Ptolemy XII married his daughter, simply that they enjoyed a joint rule.

The placement of the title "king's wife" suggests that this temple dedication at Koptos was made during Cleopatra's marriage to either Ptolemy XIII or Ptolemy XIV (Ashton in Walker and Ashton eds. 2003: 25–6), making this small fragment an important piece of evidence for the early part of her co-rule and her independence as a monarch. In a detailed publication of the monument in 1992 it was suggested that the male consort represents Ptolemy XIV (Traunecker 1992: 316–17; 322–4).

There is further evidence for such an identification in the form of a limestone crown from a statue that was found by Petrie

Plate 3.10 Limestone crown from a statue. The crown has a triple uraeus and is inscribed with the titles of the queen. Petrie Museum of Egyptian Archaeology, University College London UC 14521

during his excavations at Koptos, which award a queen, possibly Cleopatra VII, an additional title: that of "king's sister" (Plate 3.10). The crown belonged to a life-size statue of a Ptolemaic queen. The identity of the subject can be narrowed down on account of a specific iconographic feature: a triple rather than single uraeus (cobra). Arsinoe II was the sister and wife of Ptolemy II and wore two cobras on her brow; however, the type of crown seen on the Petrie example (double plume, sun-disk, and horns) is not that worn by this particular queen. Arsinoe was awarded a more elaborate crown that was sometimes borrowed by Cleopatra III and VII and not the more generic form worn by the majority of females from the dynasty. Here the crown's only distinctive feature is the triple uraeus. The text on the back of the crown is sadly lacking a name, but given the Ptolemaic tradition of repeating first names it is unlikely that this would help with the identification of the subject. The triple uraeus is associated with the double cornucopia and there are only three queens for whom it has been suggested that there was a direct link with this emblem – Arsinoe II, Cleopatra III, and Cleopatra VII. Arsinoe II consistently wore the double uraeus and so it is unlikely that artists would suddenly start to use a triple. The double cornucopia also appears on the reverse of coins minted during the reign of Cleopatra VII and on coins dating to the reign of Ptolemy VIII (Ashton 2001a: 40–3).

The re-examination of the crown by a number of scholars has reiterated the difficulties of working on the fragmentary evidence that serves the Ptolemaic period. The problem lies not in the number of surviving objects but the lack of inscriptional evidence on statues in particular. As noted the Petrie statue in the form of a crown was originally attributed to Arsinoe II on account of the find spot, the titles, and the multiple cobras. This identification has been challenged and Cleopatra VII suggested as an alternative. In response to this proposal it has been noted that the titles in the second column with the epithet Hor are attested for Ptolemy II (and thus by association Arsinoe II), but not for Cleopatra VII (Bianchi 2003: 18–19). This title, as suggested, rules out the male consort being Ptolemy XV because he did not take the full title Hor (as sole ruler). The problem remains our lack of knowledge of the cartouches of Ptolemies XIII and XIV. Bianchi concludes that the crown with the triple uraeus is that of Arsinoe II, in spite of the lack of evidence for this form of crown being associated with this particular queen. It is possible, given the confusion over titles, that they could be associated with Ptolemy XII's sons. Bianchi's point about the cultic value of titles as opposed to their reality is valid; queens who were not the sister of the king were often called so during this period. The question over the triple uraeus requires further attention.

In addition to temple dedications there is further evidence for the reign of Cleopatra in the form of a dedicatory relief commemorating the death of the Buchis bull during the reign of Augustus. Although this document was carved during the rule of Cleopatra's successor, it provides important evidence for the queen's early autonomy. The stela was commissioned in 51 BCE, when Cleopatra was ruling with Ptolemy XIII. Line 10 reads: ". . . he [the Buchis Bull] was installed by the King himself in year 1, Phamenoth 19. The Queen, the lady of the two lands (BLANK CARTOUCHE), the goddess who loves her father, (11) rowed him in the barque of Amun together with the boats of the king, all of the inhabitants of Thebes and Hermonthis and priests being with him . . ." (translation by Fairman in Mond and Myers 1934: 11–13 in Jones 2006: 35–8). Although the cartouche of Cleopatra remains blank the epithet "the goddess who loves her father" indicates that the queen was Cleopatra. It is noteworthy that she is recorded as having taken such an active cult role in the installation of the new bull and this probably reflects her power as well as her interest in Egyptian religious traditions.

Finally, a fragment of a statue, found at Fouah in the Egyptian Delta measuring 53 cm in height and preserved from the abdomen upwards (Walker and Higgs 2001: 169, no. 168) is perhaps an early image of Cleopatra VII. The chin is particularly prominent and not unlike that on an inscribed limestone statue of Ptolemy XII found at Tebtunis in the Fayoum (Ashton 2001a: 24, 86–7 no. 11; Stanwick 2002: 123, 203, E3). The Fouah statue has a youthful appearance. The eyes are almond-shaped with naturalistic eyebrows and the mouth is small and is forced into a smile; this particular feature is typical of early Ptolemaic statues. However, the drapery and chin suggest a first century date. The dress is of particular interest. The shawl is pulled into a knot between the breasts; underneath is the traditional sheath-like garment worn by royal women and goddesses. A similar costume can be seen on the gateway close to the Khonsu temple at Karnak (Plate 3.11), where Berenice II appears with her husband Ptolemy III, who wears a ceremonial cloak. It is likely that the knotted

Plate 3.11 The gateway of Khonsu, Karnak

garment worn by Berenice served a similar purpose. The appearance of this feature on the Fouah statue also suggests a ceremonial occasion, and it is possible that it was commissioned to celebrate a particular event. The knotted garment is one of the features attributed to a group of divine representations that will be discussed in chapter 6. However, the Fouah statue has the more traditional tripartite, echeloned wig with a single uraeus and does not fit easily into any of the suggested groups. The subject cannot unequivocally be identified as Cleopatra VII, but the similarity to the statue of Ptolemy XII suggests that it represents a woman with whom he was associated, perhaps Cleopatra V or her daughter Cleopatra Berenice.

3.9 PROBLEMS DURING CLEOPATRA'S EARLY RULE

The annual inundation of the river Nile was crucial for Egypt's crops and economy. Too heavy a flood or too little for a consecutive number of years resulted in disaster for a country that was entirely dependent upon the river for the cultivation of its land. The role of the king of Egypt was closely linked to the successful inundation. Respect for the annual flood was so great that rulers were forbidden to sail during the annual flood, a principle that was still firmly in place in the second century CE under Hadrian, who was emperor and so king of Egypt.

Cleopatra was unfortunate during the first year of her co-rule when there was a series of poor harvests. The food shortages that resulted from poor inundations had a much greater effect upon cities than the countryside, for the simple reason that food could be grown locally. In 50 BCE Ptolemy XIII and Cleopatra VII issued a decree in an attempt to counteract this problem. The decree dates to October 27, 50 BCE, and is the earliest form of this document from Cleopatra VII's reign. The rulers are listed with the king first (this was Ptolemy XIII) and then Cleopatra. The decree ruled that grain was only to be transported to Alexandria. The penalty for ignoring this rule was death. Furthermore, the decree states that in the event of a successful prosecution, those who informed upon the accused were to be rewarded with the property of the perpetrator. The addition of this means of encouraging people to report those who contravened the royal decree indicates the serious nature of its intention. Later that year Cleopatra's fears were realized, when there was a second low flood. Pliny notes that it was the lowest inundation on record (*Natural Histories* 5.58). As a backdrop to these natural problems there was the political unrest of the Alexandrian wars (Thompson 2003: 32–3).

Further problems continued to impede Cleopatra's rule. In 42 BCE, further low floods occurred (Seneca 4a 2.16), and, according to Appian (*Civil Wars* 4.61 and 4.63), famine and pestilence followed. On April 12, 41 BCE a further royal decree was issued. The problem now was the high taxes that were levied upon land owners. The ruling house's response was to exempt country estates from additional "Crown" taxation. This ruling was the result of pressure from the landowners in the Bubastite and Prosopite nomes (administrative centers) which were close to Alexandria and in direct contact with the ruling house (Thompson 2003: 33).

Ptolemaic gold coinage had ceased to be minted some years before Cleopatra came to power. Cleopatra did not re-introduce it. The queen initiated an important change by debasing the silver coinage early in her reign. It has been suggested that this reform pulled the Egyptian silver coinage in line with the Roman denarius. However, the production of bronze coins was reintroduced at the royal mint in Alexandria (Walker and Higgs 2001: 177). The images present Cleopatra as a Greek ruler and she is always presented alone on coinage minted in Egypt. The portrait types vary throughout her reign with a more mature image that is linked to some of her numismatic representations abroad being produced in the later part of her reign (Walker 2003b). This indicates that the economic condition of Egypt was poor. This was not entirely Cleopatra's fault. Her father had borrowed considerably from the Romans in order to assert his authority and maintain his position as king of Egypt.

3.10 JULIUS CAESAR

As noted above, Julius Caesar wrote an account of his meeting with Cleopatra in the more general sense of a narrative of his campaign. Nowhere in his accounts are there any personal references to the queen or his relationship with her. Caesar was a notorious womanizer. In Cleopatra he had found a woman who had power beyond even the imagination of Roman women at this time. We are entirely dependent upon largely later historical sources for descriptions of Caesar's relationship with Cleopatra and there are far fewer references on the subject than on Antony and Cleopatra. This is largely because of Octavian's campaign against the latter pair. Criticizing Julius Casear, Octavian's adopted "father," was less likely to obtain imperial support.

In Plutarch's *Life of Julius Caesar* Cleopatra appears in chapter 48, where Plutarch reports that some people believed Caesar's involvement in the war in Egypt to be on account of his passion for Cleopatra. We are told that Cleopatra had been driven from Egypt. In chapter 49 (*Life of Caesar*) Plutarch describes the famous return of Cleopatra with the aid of Apollodorus the Sicilian, who took the queen in a small skiff, landing at the palace and hid her in a bed-sack, not a carpet as later became the tradition (Walker and Ashton 2006: 41–2). Clearly this meeting was successful because Cleopatra was once again named as joint ruler of Egypt. She was 22, her brother, born in 61 BCE (Hölbl 2001), was 10, and her lover Julius Caesar was 30 years her senior.

Some Roman writers refer to Caesar's affection for Cleopatra. Caesar had many lovers but we are told by one author that: "most particularly he loved Cleopatra, with whom he prolonged parties until dawn, and with her, too, he journeyed by royal barge deep into Egypt, and would have reached Ethiopia but his army refused to follow him. Moreover he welcomed her to Rome and only let her go home when he had showered her with the greatest honours and gifts" (Suetonius, *Deified Julius Caesar* 52).

Other Roman writers noted these two events. It was said (Appian, *Civil Wars* 2.98), that 400 ships formed the entourage of Cleopatra and Caesar on their Nile voyage. In this way Caesar was able to assert his authority and Cleopatra was able to show the Romans her country, wealth, and power. The fact that upon his return to Rome Julius Caesar held a victory celebration (Appian 2.102) could be interpreted as evidence of a policy of a progressive foothold by which Rome would further dominate Egypt.

3.11 WHEN IN ROME

The situation in which the queen found herself in 46 BCE is peculiar even by modern standards. The queen, possibly with her illegitimate son by Julius Caesar, and her "husband" and brother Ptolemy XIV were guests of Caesar, some think in his villa on the Esquiline hill (Dio, *Roman History* 43.27.3). It has been suggested that Cleopatra made a number of trips to Rome between 46 BCE and Julius Caesar's murder in March 44 BCE rather than residing there continually (Gruen 2003: 257–74). This seems altogether a more sensible arrangement given the propensity for unrest in Alexandria during a monarch's absence.

Cleopatra was certainly not popular with the majority of Romans. Perhaps her staunchest contemporary critic was Cicero (*Atticus*). The queen appears in six of the writer's private letters. The circumstances in which she is mentioned are often not fully understood. The letters were written between April and June 44 BCE, and so after the death of Julius Caesar. Unlike many of the sources, these letters reveal a personal and private opinion of the queen, but one that was shared openly by Cicero with the Senate. Many of Cicero's references are cryptic, simply because the other half of his correspondence has not survived.

Cleopatra's departure from Rome is made reference to (*Atticus* 14. 8.1) in a letter written at on April 16, 44 BCE. Cicero wrote "The queen's flight does not distress me" (Lacey 1986: no. 362). In 14.20.2, which was written at Puteoli on May 11, 44 BCE, Cicero comments on a rumor to which Atticus must have referred by writing "I hope it is true about the queen, and about that Caesar of her's too." The nature of the rumor is not known (Lacey 1986: no. 374, 239 n.8). A week later in a letter written at Puteoli on May 17, 44 BCE (15.1.5) we are told that "the rumour about the queen is dying out." On May 24 Cicero wrote: "I wish it had been true about Menedemus. I wish it may be true about the queen" (Lacey 1986: no. 381), suggesting that the rumor was simply that. Cicero's most famous correspondence is that in which he complains about Cleopatra and her advisors, dating to mid-June 44 BCE (14.15.2): "The arrogance of the queen herself when she was living on the estate across the Tiber makes my blood boil to recall. So I want nothing to do with them. . . . I hate the queen (*reginam odi*). Ammonius, who guaranteed her promises, knows that I have the right to do so. These were of a literary kind, not unbecoming to my position – I should not mind telling them to a public meeting. As for Sara, over and above his general rascality, I found him personally insolent as well. Once and only once I saw him at my house . . ." (Lacey 1986: 393). It has been suggested (Lacey 1986: 263) that

Sara might possibly be a short version of Sarapio who was a councillor of Cleopatra's father, Ptolemy XII and who, in 48 BCE, assisted Julius Caesar against his enemies (Caesar, *Civil Wars* 3 109.4), and became Cleopatra's viceroy in Cyprus in 43 BCE. It is clear that by this time Cleopatra was no longer resident in Rome. Her departure from Roman society and so out of the immediate subject of the letters is perhaps referred to in the final mention of Cleopatra. On June 14, 44 BCE (14.17.2) Cicero wrote "I am glad that you are not worried about the queen and that you approve of my witness" (Lacey 1986: no. 394).

Archaeological traces of Cleopatra in Rome

Cleopatra's legacy to the Romans will be considered in the final chapter of this book. There are, however, traces of the queen in Rome from her visit during the lifetime of Julius Caesar. A statue representing Cleopatra and dedicated by Caesar next to the image of Venus in the temple of Venus Genetrix (Appian, *Civil Wars* 2.102) reveals a remarkable gesture. When Appian was writing in the second century CE, the statue was still in situ. We know nothing of its form, but it has been suggested that it showed Cleopatra in the form of Venus/Aphrodite and that a copy survives. Statues accompanied by snakes are often cited as copies of Cleopatra's Roman statue. However, the task of identifying the statue has not exactly been helped by the fashion of restorers adding a snake to antique statues representing female nudes (Higgs 2001: 202). The presence of a snake on the statue of Cleopatra carried in Octavian's victory parade is discussed in chapter 8. There is no other reason to suggest that the statue of Cleopatra in the temple of Venus Genetrix pictured a snake. At this point Cleopatra still had around 15 years to live and was in a strong political position.

The problem, as is always the case with Cleopatra, is that we know so little about her circumstances during her visit to Rome. We cannot say with any certainty that Ptolemy XV Caesar had already been born, but we know that Cleopatra must have been pregnant by March 44 BCE when Caesar was murdered. It was perhaps this particular maternal aspect that the queen would wish to promote during her time in Italy.

Of the two heads representing Cleopatra and from Rome, one has an interesting mark that may suggest it was accompanied by a second figure representing Ptolemy Caesar. Now in the Vatican Museums, the first head was found at the Villa dei Quintilii on the Via Appia in Rome (Higgs 2001: 203–4). The head was first identified as an image of Cleopatra VII by Curtius in 1933 (Walker and Higgs 2001: 218–19, no. 196). The methods employed in this identification were those still used by specialists in Hellenistic royal sculpture today, by using a comparison of inscribed coins portraits with larger stone representation in the round. The nose is missing and there is some discoloration of the stone, but the head is in extremely good condition. The hair is pulled back in cables forming what is known as a "melon coiffure" and at the back of the head is a bun. Wisps of hair are carved around the fringe and the nape of the neck and on the crown of the head is a *nodus* (knot) (Plate 3.12).

A second head, similar in form to the Vatican example, will also be discussed in the following chapter with regard to Cleopatra's presentation as a Greek ruler (Plate 3.13). Research has suggested that this "portrait" was manufactured in Italy (Walker and Higgs 2001: 200–1, no. 198), perhaps south of Rome. It is a controversial piece in that many believe it to be a modern forgery on account of its remarkable state of preservation (Johansen 2003). It is possible that the statue to which it originally belonged was manufactured after the queen's stay, perhaps even after her lifetime. Both representations would have served a Roman audience and it is noteworthy that Cleopatra's imagery was able to adapt so easily and that she could be presented in a number of different ways. The broad diadem, a feature of both representations, is typical of Late Hellenistic Greek royal representations and indicates that her status was that of a ruler rather than a god. The two representations are modeled on Cleopatra's Greek-style presentation on Alexandrian coinage, and like many

Plate 3.12 Marble statue of Cleopatra VII. Museo Gregoriano Profano, Vatican Museums

such representations of this period show the close relationship between the coexisting Greek and Roman worlds.

Finally, we have a representation that connects the Egyptian and Roman worlds, and which was no doubt dedicated during her stay in Rome. The image is preserved in the form of a marble head with Egyptianizing headdress and wig; it represents the goddess Isis and was no doubt housed in an Egyptian sanctuary. The representation will be discussed with regard to Cleopatra in chapter 6 below. However, the existence of an Egyptian sanctuary in Rome during the Late Republican period is noteworthy in respect to Cleopatra's presence in the city.

Following the death of Julius Caesar, Cleopatra returned to Egypt with her brother and co-ruler Ptolemy XIV. Soon after

Plate 3.13 Marble statue of Cleopatra VII. Bildarchiv Preußischer Kulturbesitz (bpk)

their arrival Cleopatra is said to have had her brother put to death (Porphyry 260f 2.16–17; Josephus, *Jewish Antiquities* 15.89; Josephus, *Against Apion* 2.58). Ptolemy XV was soon named co-ruler.

4

RULER, REGENT, AND PHARAOH

4.1 FEMALE ROLE MODELS

A distinction here must be made between women who ruled Egypt, as Cleopatra VII did, and women who had power and influence through their position as a royal wife. In earlier Egyptian society the king had many wives. From these, one would be distinguished as the principal wife of the king (Ashton 2003a: 1–2). Another important role was that of mother of the king. Both of these positions, at certain times, produced powerful women whose elevated status was recorded in sculpture and on temple reliefs. However, the majority of Egyptian royal women remained anonymous. Even when royal women were awarded a more prominent role or particular iconography to distinguish them from others, their titles were bound to the king. There is no single term for queen in Egyptian. Royal women took titles associated with the male ruler, such as "king's/great royal wife," "king's mother," "king's sister." As noted, Cleopatra herself took the same titles as recorded on a crown from Koptos (Plate 3.10). From the New Kingdom principal royal women were often associated with a god in their titulary (Troy 1986), thus awarding them some independence from their consort or son. There are two dynasties under which royal women enjoyed positions of increased status and potentially power: the eighteenth, which produced Hatshepsut, Tiye, and Nefertiti, and the twenty-fifth, when female members of the royal family adopted specific roles.

Egyptian kings (some of whom took the title pharaoh) were usually men. One of the few exceptions to this rule was

Hatshepsut who, as a female, adopted the title and uniform of the male kings of Egypt (Dorman 2005: 87–90; Roehrig ed. 2005: 164–73, no. 88–171). Hatshepsut was the daughter of King Thutmose I and the half-sister and wife of his successor Thutmose II. Her elevation to co-ruler can be tracked through her role as a "god's wife," to regent to her nephew Thutmose III, and finally to co-ruler of Egypt. She was in power from around 1473–1458 BCE. In this respect her position was similar to certain Ptolemaic queens, most notably Cleopatra III and Cleopatra VII, both of whom ruled with their sons as the dominant partner. Hatshepsut became pharaoh through her political roles as god's wife and king's mother (Dorman 2005: 87). During the early years of her regency Hatshepsut was presented as a royal woman; she often wore the plumed crown of a god's wife of Amun (Dorman 2005: 87–8, figs. 37–8). Seven years into the regency of Thutmose III Hatshepsut presented herself as the king's first daughter (Dorman 2005: 88), and adopted the appearance of a male pharaoh (Hayes 1957: 79–81). At this time Hatshepsut presented a new, more direct means of legitimizing her rule.

The presence of key women on the walls of the mortuary temple of Hatshepsut is striking; the ruler's mother appeared on the temple reliefs (Roehrig ed. 2005: 153, no. 80). There is also a depiction of another female ruler of a foreign land known as Punt; she appears with exaggerated physical malformation that, it has been suggested, might be more of a caricature than a physical likeness (Ashton and Spanel 2000). At Hatshepsut's funerary temple at Deir el Bahri on the Theban West Bank feminine aspects of her role are stressed, in particular in the chapel of Hathor (Patch 2005: 173–5). On the relief decorations of this the seated ruler feeds the goddess who appears in the form of a cow rather than in her usual human form. There is also a depiction of the pregnant ruler in the chapel of Thutmose (Arnold 2005: 135–40). Hatshepsut was also keen to promote her own daughter's status. Neferure became a "god's wife" as her mother had done before her. In her statues and on temple reliefs, as we have seen, Hatshepsut is shown in the guise of a male king of Egypt. However, her female physiognomy is represented by feminine breasts and a dress worn underneath her kilt covering her torso, according to the usual Egyptian artistic tradition. The ruler also used the female form in her titulary (Dorman 2005: 88).

Later in the eighteenth Dynasty two powerful and prominent women overlapped. They were Tiye, wife of Amenhotep III and mother of the king Amenhotep IV/Akhenaten, and her daughter-in-law Nefertiti. These two royal women compare well to the queens of the Ptolemaic dynasty (Ashton 2003a: 6–10), with respect to the roles they fulfilled and the iconography adopted to differentiate the pair from other royal women. Tiye came to prominence when she ruled as consort to the king. The number of statues representing her both alone and with her husband far exceeds those of earlier royal wives. Following the death of Amenhotep III, Tiye seems to continue in a dominant role as mother of the king, allowing Nefertiti to take over the role of royal wife. Their position is closest to that of the early Ptolemaic queens, particularly Arsinoe II, whose divinity and prominence depended on her association with her brother Ptolemy II. Later Ptolemaic queens surpassed this dependency and ruled in their own right and, on occasion, were preferred over the contemporary males of the dynasty.

Other women who attempted to seize power were often quashed by courtiers. One such example was the nineteenth-Dynasty principal wife of Sety II (Ashton 2003a: 13). Like many other women who had ambitions beyond their perceived status, Tauseret was replaced by a young child, who would have been easier to manipulate. The episode reveals a very real caution on behalf of members of the royal court. Women may have had their place in Egyptian society but it seems that they were considered to be a genuine threat rather than an easy and easily manipulated alternative to a male king.

The twenty-fifth Dynasty were foreign rulers from the kingdom of Kush and are often called Kushites. Kush is in Nubia and was traditionally seen to be an enemy of Egypt. Thus, in smiting scenes the king of Egypt is often seen crushing enemies of the state, one of which is shown as a Black African and representing the Nubians (a culture identified by a common language from the region, today identified as Southern Egypt and Sudan). As foreign pharaohs the Kushites ruled about 400 years before the Ptolemies. Like the Ptolemaic rulers the Kushites seem to have been genuinely interested in Egyptian culture and in promoting themselves as kings of Egypt in a traditional manner.

Similarities can be found in the adoption of African features on representations of the Kushite kings and the adoption of Greek-style "portraits" for statues of Ptolemaic rulers (Ashton 2001a: 25–36). The royal women of this period were also given important and dominant positions both religious and political and as such provide a legitimate comparison with Ptolemaic queens. Of this dynasty Amenirdas I, sister of the ruler Piye (747–716 BCE) and aunt of his successor, is notable. Amenirdas, like many prominent women before her, was given the role of "god's wife of Amun," in which a royal female became a divine consort of the god at Thebes. As the consort of Amun, Amenirdas was given financial rewards and thus political power. Like Hatshepsut before her, Amenirdas is thought to have selected her successor as "god's wife of Amun," her niece Shepenwepet (Markoe and Capel eds. 1997: 115–16, no. 48). The God's Wives appear on the chapel associated with their funerary cults at Medinat Habu (Plate 4.1), and it is not difficult to see where the Ptolemaic priests might have turned for inspiration when representing Cleopatra's ancestors. The relief decoration of this temple shows the deeply personal link between the women. The only male figures are gods, and the scenes show the current wife offering to the divine former consort. Such scenes would be repeated in the Ptolemaic period where rulers were shown offering to their deceased and divine parents. On the inner walls of the first sanctuary are representations of worshippers bringing offerings to the statues of the deified royal wife (Plate 4.2).

4.2 PTOLEMAIC ICONOGRAPHY

The Egyptian priesthood turned to images of earlier royal women when the need for a distinctive iconography became apparent

Plate 4.1 Chapel of the God's Wives of Amun, Medinat Habu

Plate 4.2 Chapel of the God's Wives of Amun, Medinat Habu, detail

early in the new dynasty. There had been a number of prominent royal women during the eighteenth, nineteenth, and twenty-fifth dynasties. As seen in Plate 4.3, Arsinoe II wore a specific type of headdress based on the crown of the god Geb (Dils 1998: 1309–30). This iconography remained consistent throughout the Ptolemaic period, as illustrated by posthumous representations of the queen. Consistency in the attributes used to identify Ptolemaic queens was important because of the lack of inscriptions on statuary and the number of blank cartouches on temple reliefs. The setting up of royal images as described in the Canopus and Rosetta decrees is detailed and would have aided recognition and distinction between rulers most importantly in a temple-sharing capacity (Ashton 2001a: 13–19 for summary). Fortunately there are two inscribed Egyptian-style statues of Arsinoe II: one showing the queen as one of the Theoi Adelphoi from during her lifetime, the other a posthumous, probably second-century-BCE, representation of the queen, now in the Metropolitan Museum of Art, New York (Plate 4.3) (Ashton 2001a: 37–8, cat. 54 108–9 and cat. 35 100–1; 2001b: cat. 166, 166–7). The former shows the queen with a double uraeus and the latter, which has Greek attributes, shows the queen with a parallel double horn of plenty (Ashton 2000:4). The uraeus was usually single in form and was a symbol of solar kingship but also, in the case of the royal women, possibly associated them with the goddess Wadjet and more generally with the daughter of Ra as in mythology.

The double uraeus appeared on images of royal women from the Eighteenth Dynasty; one cobra wears the crown of Upper Egypt and the other the crown of Lower Egypt, thus together symbolizing their unification (Griffiths 1961: 50–1; Russmann 1974: 39; Robins 1996: 24). In the case of Arsinoe II, the double uraeus complements the double cornucopia and both may have had a similar meaning. The title Mistress of the Two Lands can be associated with some of the uses of the double uraeus (Ashton 2005a: 4). This was the case for Arsinoe II and the Eighteenth Dynasty wife of Amenhotep III and mother of Akhenaten, Tiye.

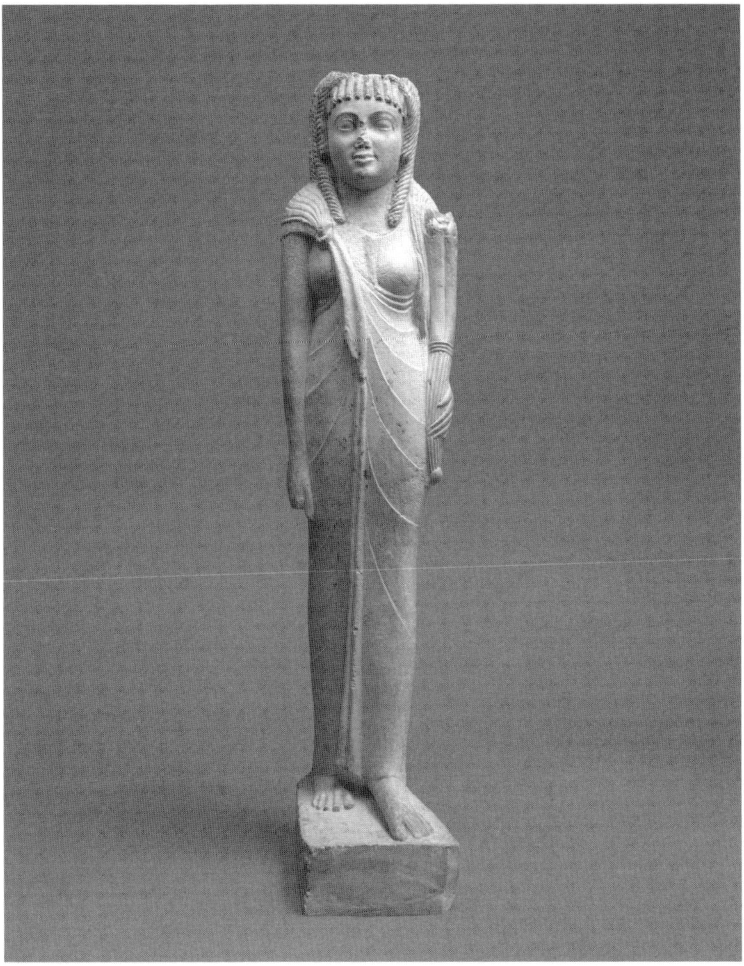

Plate 4.3 Limestone statue of Arsinoe II. The Metropolitan Museum of Art, New York, 1920 (20.2.21). Image © The Metropolitan Museum of Art

The iconography that Tiye adopted as principal wife, notably a double rather than single uraeus was passed on to her successor Nefertiti. This can be seen on a statue that originally had two cobras but was altered to support a single cobra, presumably on account of her new status as mother and not wife of the king (Arnold 1996: 30–5). Even during the first part of her first rule, Tiye is shown not only as a royal wife but also as a goddess. Many of her statues dating from the reign of Amenhotep III show Tiye with a double uraeus (distinguishing her) and with a central vulture (indicating her divinity). In early statues and temple reliefs Nefertiti likewise is shown with the double uraeus (Ashton 2005a: 1–2). The cobras support single examples of the crowns of Upper and Lower Egypt, representing the Two Lands (Ashton 2005a: 5). It has also been suggested that the double cobras were used to commemorate a specific event during the reign of royal women. For Tiye this would have been the Heb Sed festival, a festival of renewal, which was normally celebrated after 30 years of a king's rule. Not all rulers waited 30 years; Akhenaten held a Heb festival three years into his reign. Although Nefertiti wore two cobras early in her reign, the appearance is sporadic if the current dating of examples is accepted (Ashton 2005a: 6). The double cobras that are found on reliefs and statues of Nefertiti do not support crowns of Upper and Lower Egypt, but rather cow's horns and a sun-disk. This particular decoration is also found on statues dating to the Twenty-fifth Dynasty and it has been suggested that the motif is associated with the goddess Hathor and her association with royal women (Ashton 2005a: 6). As previously noted, many of these women took the role of God's wife and often took the divine titles of *S3t Imn*, *S3t Re* or *S3t G'b* (Daughter of Amun, Re or Geb). It should be noted that Hathor herself is not associated with the double cobras.

Once adopted, the majority of royal women retained the double form of uraeus. An exception to this rule, as just noted, is Nefertiti, who returned to the single form, later in her reign. The return to the single uraeus coincided with Nefertiti's own promotion as the agent through whom the Aten (sun-disk) could be worshipped as part of the religious developments during this short period. During this time the worship of the Aten dominated but was not exclusive. Both Tiye and Nefertiti clearly played an important political role within the court and the latter was an important component of the new focus for religion in that the Aten was worshipped through Akhenaten and Nefertiti.

Some scholars have suggested that these seemingly powerful women were instrumental in the developments of the Amarna period.

In an article dated to 2003 it was suggested in a somewhat simplistic overview by a classical scholar that the two cobras and double cornucopia of Arsinoe II represented her rule with her brother (Maehler 2003). The problem with this hypothesis is that it lacks valid support. The very fact that the double uraeus reappears in the Ptolemaic period suggests that the priests were aware of its earlier use and understood its previous uses. It is unfortunate that the example that was cited to illustrate this theory – the pair of statues of Arsinoe II and Ptolemy II now in the Vatican Museums (Ashton 2001a: 84 cat. 6 and 100 cat. 36) – are actually part of a triad (Ashton 2007a). A PhD study published in 2002 concluded, in contrast, that the two cobras could be linked to the title of Mistress of the Two Lands, as suggested above (Ashton 2005a, presented in 2001; Albersmeier 2002: 44–52). Whilst this explains the cobras with crowns, and also those women who are associated with this title, it will not explain all examples of the phenomenon. It seems that women wearing multiple cobras were those who needed to be distinguished in some way. This idea is a logical one given the number of wives a king of Egypt would take, and the motif seems to have been used by women at key times during their reign. I would conclude that the double uraeus was used to identify, or differentiate between, the principal wife or daughter of the king (Ashton 2005a: 6–8). Arsinoe II needed to be distinguished from Arsinoe I and so the double uraeus must have been an obvious solution to those advising the royal household. It is highly probable that the motif was used for different purposes at different times. Certainly, there is no link between titles and its use.

The Ptolemaic period saw the appearance of a triple uraeus for the first time in Egyptian royal iconography. There has been much debate over the significance of this and also with whom this attribute can be associated. In the Cleopatra exhibition of 2000 it was suggested that the triple uraeus might represent a number of circumstances: a triple rule, the titles king's daughter,

Plate 4.4 Steatite statue representing Cleopatra VII. Musée du Louvre, Paris, inv. E 13102

king's sister, great royal wife as found on the aforementioned Petrie Museum crown from Koptos (see Plate 3.10), or the title queen of kings (Ashton 2001b: 148–55 and Ashton 2001a: 40–3). Some specialists of Ptolemaic royal sculpture prefer to see the triple uraeus as an extension of Arsinoe II's iconography (Bianchi 2003: 18–19), while others conclude that some statues represent Cleopatra VII (Stanwick 2002: E13–15, F5), but prefer to date some more widely to the first century BCE (Stanwick 2002: E11) and the reign of Cleopatra III (Stanwick 2002: 37, 76, 80, no's. E 13–15, F5 and E 11). One scholar prefers to maintain a traditional date of the third century BCE for some of the group whilst dating the Louvre statue (Plate 4.4) to the first century BCE (Albersmeier 2002: 44–5). Analysis on stylistic grounds is more sensible than seeing the triple uraeus as a representation of a triple rule of Cleopatra II with her brothers Ptolemy VI and Ptolemy VIII, or with her daughter Cleopatra III and Ptolemy VIII (Maehler 2003: 302). Having now had time to consider responses to the British Museum exhibition where it was suggested that the triple uraeus was solely linked to Cleopatra VII, and having undertaken further research on the use of multiple uraei and their use in royal iconography (Ashton 2001a; 2005a), I remain convinced that the statues with a triple uraeus can be linked to Cleopatra VII on iconographic as well as stylistic grounds. The identification, however, and meaning of this motif will no doubt continue to be debated.

The usual crown worn by Ptolemaic queens consisted of double plumes with a sun-disk and cow's horns, thus promoting Hathoric aspects of the queen as earlier royal females had done (Robins 1996: 24). Some queens wore a vulture crown to indicate their divinity, most notably Tiye, the Kushite god's wives of Amun during their lifetime, and Arsinoe II in her posthumous cult statues. On wall reliefs, Arsinoe II also wore a vulture headdress when receiving a cult offering. Queens usually appear making an offering to a god and as such wear the single royal cobra on their brow.

4.3 CLEOPATRA AS RULER

Chapter 3 considered the early years of Cleopatra's rule with her father and then her brothers. The remainder of this chapter will look at the development of her role as ruler of Egypt following the death of Julius Caesar in 44 BCE. Cleopatra's relationship with Mark Antony will be discussed further in chapter 7. Although they fathered her children, it has been suggested that there was no place for the Romans within the Egyptian royal tradition (Maehler 1983). That is not to say that Cleopatra was not mindful of the two men. A temple to the deified Julius Caesar in Alexandria indicates that Caesar played a role both politically and sentimentally in the development of the second part of her reign. It has also, more recently, been suggested that the queen targeted specific deities in order to emulate her own unconventional situation (Ray 2003: 9–11).

Cleopatra's rule with her father secured her position as ruler of Egypt. His decision to leave the country jointly to his daughter and his elder son was politically astute. If the country had been left solely to Cleopatra it is likely that courtiers would have seized the opportunity under the name of Ptolemy XIII to take control of the country. Even with the right to rule the country firmly secured, Cleopatra was forced into exile when the supporters of her young consort did precisely what her father had probably feared. The civil war that ensued gave the Romans the perfect opportunity to interfere further and secure a formal role in the running of the country. As noted previously, the Egyptians seem to have had no problem with being ruled by a woman and the Alexandrians had accepted earlier Ptolemaic queens, in the case of Cleopatra II preferring them to the male opposition (see chapter 3). It was, however, the Romans who seem to have been more disturbed with the idea of a female monarch.

4.4 CLEOPATRA'S *PHILOI*, ADVISORS AND PRIESTS

Although there is scant documentary evidence for the reign of Cleopatra VII, statues of some of the queen's officials have survived (Walker and Higgs 2001: 180–3). The first represents a man named "Pa-ashem," who was the governor of Denderah around 50–30 BCE (Bianchi 1988: 127). The surface of the statue was unfinished; the text, however, is complete. Egyptian sculptors do not seem always to have finished off the surfaces of statues, often leaving key features such as the hands or feet in what we consider an unfinished state. This particular statue was perhaps dedicated by the official himself, or on his behalf. The titles on the back pillar suggest (Walker and Higgs 2001: 181) that the governor acted in a priestly role as "prophet of the statues of the pharaoh," "guardian of the treasure of Horus of Edfu," "prophet of Isis at Denderah and Isis at Philae" etc. The last line of text gives the name and occupation of Pa-ashem's father, a man named Pa-srj, who was a general.

Another official of Cleopatra's to be represented was a man named Hor, who was priest of Thoth (Walker and Higgs 2001: 182–3). This statue was found in Alexandria. The subject appears on a relief scene, offering to Thoth who was scribe to the gods. In this role Hor is shown with his head shaved, as part of the usual cleansing ritual before approaching a deity. On the statue, however, he appears with a head of short curls. During his lifetime Hor rebuilt a temple to the god Osiris, which had fallen into ruin due to the building of a canal close by. The third line of text on the back pillar states that Hor looked after the divine offerings to the god Amun-Ra. This suggests that the dedication to Hor was a personal one, or that he possibly changed priestly roles during his lifetime. The statue is an arresting representation with a "portrait" of a man who appears to be in his late forties to mid-fifties, with lines creasing his mouth and chin and around his eyes. This type of non-idealized representation was typical of officials in the Ptolemaic and early Roman periods.

4.5 DOCUMENTARY EVIDENCE FOR CLEOPATRA'S EGYPT

Unfortunately, few documents have survived from Cleopatra's reign; those that have were re-used as cartonnage wrapping for mummies of the period. Royal ordinances can be divided into three main types: general edicts, which are not addressed to an individual; instructions to an official with his title; and instructions to an official who is addressed only by his name (van Minnen 2003: 35). Some of these documents exist in their original papyrus form, others only in stone copies. This explains the process of government with instructions passing from royal decree to an official, who then instigated a stone version for others to see. The third type of edict, that addressed to a named individual, seems only to appear during the reign of Cleopatra VII, possibly during the joint rule with her father (van Minnen 2003: 35), and is a noteworthy development in the ways in which rulers communicated with their supporters. The name given to the role of office held by the addressee (the man in charge of the *procheira*) in two letters sent by Cleopatra is one that did not appear until the late Ptolemaic period, perhaps suggesting that it was introduced in order to deal with this new type of royal ordinance (van Minnen 2003: 36).

Asylum decrees to temples dating from the reign of Cleopatra VII

Temple asylum decrees first appear during the reign of Ptolemy X (Rigsby 1996: 544). Although traditionally viewed as evidence for the weakening power of the state, some have proposed that these grants were a way of smaller, less powerful temples reasserting their traditional rights. It has also been argued that, rather than simply being indicative of problems between those in competition of royal benefits and the priesthood and the royal house, the decrees signify disputes between those in competition with one another (Heinen 1994: 157–68). Asylum requests were lodged by many different members of the Ptolemaic populace in respect of Egyptian gods, by Greeks in respect of Egyptian gods, Greek gods and, in one instance, the Jewish god (Rigsby 1996: 544). There are a number from the reign of Cleopatra VII (for texts see Rigsby 1996: 569–73; Thompson 2003; and van Minnen 2003). The earliest date to March 7 and 14, 46 BCE, and comes from the temple of Isis near Ptolemais. Ptolemais was a Greek polis (city) established early in the Ptolemaic period under Ptolemies I or II and it had the same privileges as Alexandria. The petition is made by a Greek. The goddess Isis is, of course, part of the traditional Egyptian pantheon. The text is addressed to the official only by name rather than office. The text reads:

> (A) Theon to the city of the Ptolemaeans, greetings: subjoined is a copy of the proclamation transmitted to us together with the command in response, so that you may know it and deposit it in

> your public archives as is fitting. Taking care of yourselves, that you be well, farewell. Year 6, Phamenoth 12. (B) To Theon: let the relevant persons be told that the temple of Isis built on behalf of our well-being by Callimachus the *epistrategos* south of Ptolemais is to be tax-free and inviolable together with the houses built around it as far as the wall of the city. (C) Let it be done. Year 6, Phamenoth 5.

This decree was inscribed on a granite stela, now housed in a Russian collection (Rigsby 1996: 569). It is 99 centimeters high and 56 centimeters wide; the lettering is between 2–2.5 centimeters high. The decree shows the means through which an authorization was petitioned and obtained. The speed with which the request was authorized, a week, perhaps reflects the special status of Ptolemais, even though the temple was outside the city walls (Rigsby 1996: 570–1). The swift orchestration also suggests that Theon was in Alexandria in order to obtain royal permission in the form of the phrase "let it be done" and a date.

Another document refers to a synagogue, possibly at Leontopolis in the Delta, and dates to the co-rule of Cleopatra and Ptolemy XV (Rigsby 1996: 571–2, after Bingen 1995). The stela is said to be made from calcite (Rigsby 1996: 572), although this would be extremely unusual. The major part of the text is in Greek, but there is an additional sentence in Latin reading "the queen and the king have commanded" (Rigsby 1996: 573). The Greek section contains an unusual inscription concerning the replacement of a previous foundation plaque, dedicated at a synagogue during the reign of "Ptolemy Euergetes," which could be either Ptolemy III or VIII. The use of Latin suggests that the instigators were Roman; Rigsby suggests men from Antony's army. The fact that the place of worship was not a temple relevant to the queen's position or power illustrates that, as a ruler, she was concerned with all of her population (Thompson 2003: 33).

The other asylum documents dated to the reign of Cleopatra VII are only partially preserved. The first is now housed in the Museum of the University of Rome (Rigsby 1996: 571). The second is an Egyptian-style stela showing a traditional offering scene by the ruler to the god Thoth (Rigsby 1996: 573).

As noted, such decrees allow us an insight into how Cleopatra's government functioned: that, rather than writing individually to the 50 Nomes (administrative capitals) of Egypt, a trusted official was addressed directly by name and not position, and it was assumed that he would then ensure that the legislation was disseminated on the ruler's behalf (van Minnen 2003: 34–6). Scribes were employed to write such letters, but it has recently been suggested that the Queen herself must have signed such a document and that the recipient would know his ruler's signature (van Minnen 2003: 37–9). One such example has come to light – a papyrus that had formed part of mummy casing at the Hellenistic cemetery of Abusir el-Melek, discovered in the early 1900s but only read and published more recently (van Minnen 2000: 29–34). Van Minnen has argued that the instruction "let it happen" was written by Cleopatra herself. Many papyrologists dispute this claim, although van Minnen reiterated his arguments for the signature being that of the monarch in 2003. Whether or not this papyrus, which is dated to 33 BCE, was signed by Cleopatra is really of little significance beyond having an example of her writing.

The contents of the document are extremely important for our knowledge of the administration during this period. In it, Cleopatra awards substantial tax privileges to a Roman general named Publius Canidius, who was one of Mark Antony's closest allies. Canidius was allowed to export 10,000 sacks of wheat from Egypt and was awarded a licence to import 5,000 amphorae of Cretan wine into the country without paying duty (Walker and Higgs 2001: 180). The Roman was also exempt from paying taxes on the land that he owned in Egypt and this exemption was extended to his tenants. Cleopatra was clearly attempting to obtain support and allegiance from this influential Roman.

In her 2003 contribution to *Cleopatra Reassessed* Thompson discussed the titles awarded to Cleopatra in a Greek contract dating to her seventeenth year in which she is called "Cleopatra Thea Neotera, Philopator, Philopatris" (Thompson 2003: 31–4). These titles translate as "Cleopatra the New Goddess, Father-loving, who loves her country." Some scholars had suggested that the country was Egypt, others that Cleopatra's "patris" was Macedonian Greece (Thompson 2003: 31; Bingen 2007: 58–62). Thompson concludes from the scant surviving documentary evidence that Cleopatra considered Egypt to be her home and that during her rule she strove to protect that country and to rebuild its strength. Concessions such as those to Canidius were of course made, but these can be interpreted as attempts to obtain support for her vision. Certainly the archaeological evidence supports the idea that Cleopatra saw herself as an Egyptian and promoted herself wholly in this form when she was in her home country. In spite of her relationships with Caesar and more especially Mark Antony, Cleopatra held on to her son's position as her co-ruler and heir.

4.6 CLEOPATRA AS A MALE PHARAOH

The concept of Egyptian kingship was of a divine intermediary between mortals and the gods. In addition to this long-standing conception, the Ptolemaic rulers and their consorts had established further divine roles to enhance their position amongst both Greeks and Egyptians (see chapter 6).

A relief representation dedicated on behalf of "Queen Cleopatra, Father-loving Goddess" shows a male pharaoh offering to Isis and Horus above the text (Walker and Higgs 2001: 156, no. 154). This stela was originally interpreted as an example of Cleopatra in the guise of a male pharaoh; however, the poor fit of the lettering and the apparent re-cutting of the stone around the inscription have been cited as proof that the stela was re-cut and so re-used. This stela was dedicated on behalf of Cleopatra and was not an official royal decree. Whether the queen would have allowed such an image to be used in an official capacity seems questionable. Cleopatra's image seems to have been carefully controlled (Ashton 2003d: 25–30). If Cleopatra was presented as a male pharaoh, the demotic stela in the British Museum with two representations of a male pharaoh accompanied by a blank cartouche could represent the queen rather than

Plate 4.5 Basalt statue of Cleopatra III. Kunsthistorisches Museum, Wien

her son Ptolemy Caesar. It should, however, be noted that Cleopatra appears on temple reliefs with her son in the guise of a queen and not as a male pharaoh. Adopting a masculine role, in the way that Cleopatra III adopted a masculine portrait type, would be somewhat incongruous for a queen who presented herself as her son's guardian and associated herself with the goddess Isis, mother of Horus (with whom the reigning king was associated). In Egypt, following the birth of her son, Cleopatra continually stressed her role as mother of the king (Ashton 2003d: 26–9).

More recently, another stela has been found that shows Cleopatra VII in the guise of a male pharaoh (Warmenbol 2006: 205–6, no. 46; Clarysse forthcoming 2007).[1] Now housed in a Chinese collection, the stela seems to be unfinished. The offering scene shows a male ruler wearing a kilt and the crowns of Upper and Lower Egypt, offering the hieroglyphic sign for "field" to a recumbent lion on an altar. Above the head of the ruler is a cartouche spelling the name "Cleopatra." There is a demotic (cursive form of hieroglyphs) inscription below the scene in an area that was clearly intended to receive a larger dedicatory inscription. In its publication, Clarysse noted the difference in depth and quality of carving of the scene and the texts. This observation could of course be explained by two different hands: one to produce the decorative scene and a second carving the inscription. However, the large space beneath the offering scene suggests that the two elements were not part of the same phase and that the scene was carved independently of the dedication. The Demotic text reads: "the house of the burial of the (divine) lion" (Clarysse 2007). If the stela is in its original form, it provides an important development in our knowledge of how the last Ptolemaic queen was presented. The dedicant clearly felt that it was acceptable to add the cartouche of Cleopatra to a representation of a male ruler in the same way as the Louvre stela was re-used. I remain unconvinced that Cleopatra VII presented herself in an official capacity as a male ruler, however if images of earlier male rulers were adopted in an unofficial capacity by her subjects there was clearly an acceptance of her presentation in this way.

4.7 NAMES AND TITLES

Some modern scholars have suggested that Cleopatra's Egyptian titles were no more than a gesture to the Egyptian priesthood (Chauveau 2000: 46; Tait 2003 for comment). However, Egyptian royal women, with the exception of those of Amarna, were only usually given one name (their birth name), which would appear in a single cartouche (Tait 2003b: 3–8). Some of the Ptolemaic queens, including Cleopatra VII, took a Horus name in addition to their own. A Horus name was the first of five names adopted by a ruling male king. In this respect the use of this long-standing tradition for a ruling female was quite remarkable and indicates, as Tait concludes, that the Egyptian priesthood adopted an innovative approach to presenting their new rulers.

Cleopatra's decision to retain the title Philopator (father-loving) from her initial co-rule with her father was not the usual Ptolemaic practice. Rulers typically changed their names according to their new consort. In the case of Cleopatra II, she began her rule as Philometor (mother-loving), which was the name of her first consort and brother Ptolemy VI, and became Euergetes (doer-of-good-deeds) when she married her younger brother Ptolemy VIII. She reverted back to her former title when she seized control of the throne, only to continue as a Euergetes when she returned to the throne with Ptolemy VIII and her daughter. Cult titles were, therefore, a means of promoting a religious status but also a way to affirm an individual's political position. By retaining the reference to her father, fortuitously in the form of father-loving, Cleopatra was able to stress her right to rule.

The Egyptian titles adopted by Cleopatra VII are traditional and mostly linked to those of earlier royal women; many are feminine versions of masculine titles and several are directly relevant to the queen's role and positions. The royal titles are as follows:

- "The Female Horus" (Troy 1986: D2/18; 139–44). Horus was the god with whom the living king was associated and whom the king represented as a living embodiment on earth. The female version of Horus was associated with the role of regent (Troy 1986: 115–44) and had been adopted by earlier Ptolemaic queens (Ashton 2003a: 112–13). The terms *ḫkrt* "Ruler" (Troy 1986: D2/10) *ḫkrt nt3* "Ruler of the Land" (Troy 1986: D2/11) are also both female forms of male titles.
- "Noble woman" (Troy 1986: D2/1; 133–34). This translation is a loose one and does not really represent the importance or power of the title, which also had a masculine form that was used as an epithet for the creator god Geb, when acting as an intermediate between Seth and Horus (Troy 1986: 133).

It has been suggested that the feminine form of this title should be associated with the position of priestess of the god Geb and the role of a royal women as regents. It is not difficult to see why the title *rt-p't* was relevant to Cleopatra VII, who also used the epithet "Daughter of Geb" (chapter 6) and was of course regent and co-ruler with her son Ptolemy XV.

- "Mistress of the two lands" (Troy 1986: D2/14; 133–8). This title equates the role of queen to that of King, who rules the two lands and maintains a concept of Ma'at (order within the Egyptian cosmos). The title was associated with the domain of the mother of the king in a hymn dedicated to a Seventeenth Dynasty royal daughter and wife Ahhotep I (Troy 1986: 135). The role of mother of the king was dominant during the second half of Cleopatra VII's reign. The title "Lady of the South and the North" (Troy 1986: D1/4) falls under a related heading and is another way in which to assert control over Egyptian territory. "Upper Egyptian queen of the land of the White Crown, Lower Egyptian queen of the Land of the Red Crown" (Troy 1986: D3/10) also represents the feminine form of a powerful and traditional male title. The unification of the Two Lands of Upper and Lower Egypt was an important role of the ruling king.
- "Great of praises" *wrt ḥswt* (B4/11) is associated with the ceremonial role of chantress. Also associated with the role of priestess is the title "Great one of the *ḥts* sceptre" (Troy 1986: B3/6; 83–5). It is suggested that the *ḥts* scepter, which appears as a title in the Middle Kingdom and continued through the New Kingdom into the Late Period, was linked to the role of Hathor and the right of women to rule (Troy 1986: 83). In its form, the scepter is smaller than many shown on temple reliefs. It appears on representations of royal women from the Eighteenth Dynasty alongside the uraeus, diadem, and side-lock (Troy 1986: 84 fig. 55). The scepter was not exclusively associated with royal women. On the contrary, the *ḥts* ceremony was linked to the king. "Mistress of beauty of the palace courtyard" (Troy 1986: A4/10) is linked to the role of priestess (Troy 1986: 96).

4.8 PRIESTESS

In addition to the priestly titles used by Cleopatra VII there are numerous images on temple reliefs showing the queen in her role as offerant. On temple reliefs Cleopatra appears, as do earlier Ptolemaic royal women, standing behind her male consort, her son. This change from the earlier autonomy was doubtless because there was no longer a power struggle. Cleopatra was the rightful ruler and her son was her male consort, to whom she acted as regent. On the temple reliefs we see Cleopatra as priestess and official serving the gods. Her crowns are of the usual form worn by Ptolemaic queens before her: sun-disk, double plumes, and cow's horns. On the upper walls of the inner sanctuary at Denderah, however, we see Cleopatra appearing in the crown of Arsinoe II. The power is shared with that of her son Ptolemy XV, who often appears alone.

4.9 EGYPTIAN-STYLE STATUES OF CLEOPATRA VII

A number of statues have been identified as representations of Cleopatra VII through stylistic and iconographic analysis. Not all scholars agree over the designations and some prefer to suggest one or more alternative identities for individual statues. The very fact that this is in question indicates how closely linked the associated iconographies of Ptolemaic queens were. The alternative suggested identifications are Cleopatra III and Arsinoe II; both queens were role models for Cleopatra VII (Ashton 2001a: 148–53). Only the statues representing Cleopatra as a ruler are discussed here; for the other statues of Cleopatra VII as a goddess, see chapter 6.

Egyptian-style statues of Ptolemaic royal women fall into two categories: firstly those with Greek-style attributes such as corkscrew locks of hair, a cornucopia (horn of plenty), and a styling of the drapery that some consider Hellenized (Ashton 2000). The second group are closer to statues that had been produced in Egypt for several millennia. This second group represent the Ptolemaic queens as rulers, as indicated by their use on temple reliefs and the majority of statues in the round. Some of this group of statues develop with respect to the portraits. As a general rule, in the third century BCE the sculpted faces of queens imitate those of the male ruler, which in turn continued the styles of the Thirtieth Dynasty (Ashton 2004b: 544). This style continued in some workshops into the first century BCE, as indicated by a statue of Cleopatra VII as Isis (Ashton 2004b review). This observation would account for the large number of male statues with these features. As noted in chapter 3, there are a few representations of male rulers that borrow the Greek-style portrait features and often show hair beneath the headdress (Ashton 2001a: 25–36; Stanwick 2002: 47–50). These statues are a clever and effective means of transmitting a bicultural message (Ashton 2001a: 32–4). Representations of royal women continued to mimic the "portrait" features of their consorts, as indicated by the aforementioned statue of Arsinoe II dating to the reign of Ptolemy VIII, which copies the bloated face associated with this Ptolemy (Plate 4.3; Ashton 2001a: 47, 108–9, no. 54; Stanwick 2002: 117; 190, C28). The statues considered below have been dated on account of their stylistic features and in some cases on account of the triple form of uraeus.

A traditional Egyptian-style statue with a single borrowed Greek feature is now housed in the Hermitage Museum in St. Petersburg (Ashton 2001a: 48, 114–15, no. 63; Stanwick 2002: 76, D10). This statue (Plate 4.6) was instrumental in the identification of statues with a triple uraeus as representations of Cleopatra VII (Walker and Higgs 2001: 160–1, no. 160). The statue, which is carved from basalt, has a Greek cornucopia in its left hand, not the usual single one, but a double cornucopia. As noted earlier, the double cornucopia was associated with Arsinoe II as a direct parallel to the double uraeus. The Hermitage statue, in contrast, has three cobras decorating its brow. It seems unlikely that artists would use both the double and triple uraeus to represent Cleopatra VII on account of the careful

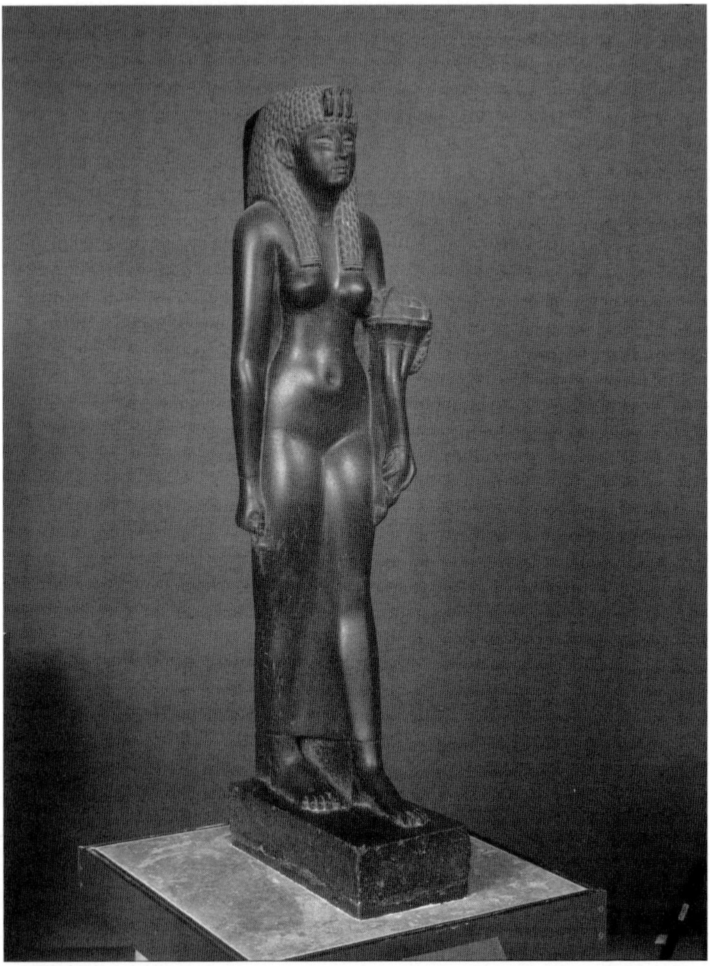

Plate 4.6 Basalt statue of Cleopatra VII. State Hermitage Museum, St. Petersburg

measures to ensure continuity that are indicated in decrees and by models that were used in workshops (Ashton 2001a: 26; Stanwick 2002: 90–3). The statue was, however, originally identified as a representation of Arsinoe II on account of the double cornucopia, and some scholars still believe that it may represent

Plate 4.7 Copper Alloy coin showing Cleopatra VII and Ptolemy Caesar as a child. The Fitzwilliam Museum Cambridge CM

this queen. Cleopatra VII also used a double cornucopia on the back of coins minted to celebrate the birth of her son Ptolemy XV (Plate 4.7). Furthermore the statue can be dated stylistically to the end of the Ptolemaic period. The down-turned mouth and pointed chin are both features also found on statues of Ptolemy XII, as noted in relation to a statue that was possibly associated with Cleopatra VII from Fouah in the Egyptian Delta. The Hermitage queen wears a tripartite, echeloned wig and the back pillar is unusually raised to a point that is almost parallel to the top of the head, a feature shared with other statues in the triple uraeus group (Ashton 2001a: 114–17). This statue is just over 1 meter in height and is extremely well carved. In the right hand is the ankh, a sign that represents the giving of life and one that can be seen on numerous relief representations in temples. The swollen abdomen and rounded thighs are doubtless a reference to fertility and echo the meaning of the cornucopia with reference to the queen's role as provider. The sheath-like dress is only really apparent at the neckline, around the wrists and just above the ankles. As was usual, the queen is shown barefoot.

Plate 4.8 Basalt statue of Cleopatra VII. Rosicrucian Museum, San Jose, California

Another statue, this time wholly Egyptian in terms of its iconography, is now housed in the Rosicrucian Museum in San Jose, California (Plate 4.8) (Ashton 2001a: 41, 102–3, no. 39; Stanwick 2002: 76, 118, D9). The statue is the same scale and roughly the same height as the Hermitage queen. Enigmatic bars are held in her clenched fists (a space filler which was commonly found on Egyptian sculpture). The subject wears a tripartite, echeloned wig, and there are three cobras on the brow. The face has the same features as the Hermitage statue, down-turned mouth and prominent chin, but the face is a little more mature in its appearance. The dress is indicated around the neck and ankles (the feet are restored), and at the elbow. The rings around the neck are known as Venus rings and suggest beauty and prosperity; in simple terms that the subject was physically rounded and could afford to eat well. Like the Hermitage statue the stomach is swollen and has a clear "doughnut ring," as art historians call the fleshy upper abdomen.

Finally, also from this group is another purely Egyptian-style statue, devoid of Greek features, that is now housed in the Louvre Museum, Paris (Plate 4.4 Walker and Higgs 2001: 163, no. 162; Ashton 2001a: 41, 102–3, cat. 40; Stanwick 2002: 76, 122, D26–Cleopatra III). The statue was discovered during research for the Cleopatra exhibition in 2000. It is carved in what appears to be steatite, a stone commonly used in the late Ptolemaic and early Roman periods in Egypt. It is wholly Egyptian in style. The lower section is missing but a drawing made when the statue was still housed in a French private collection shows a more complete version of the statue. The lower section could of course have been a restoration; the dowel hole, where the lower section was joined is still visible on the statue. The subject wears the usual wig and triple uraeus, but on top of the head is a circlet of cobras, which would have formed the base of a crown. It is 36.5 centimeters high and so would have been just under the size of the other two examples. It differs in that the queen holds a lily scepter in her left hand, which is drawn across her abdomen and allows the scepter to follow the line of her left forearm. The down-turned mouth has fleshier lips than the other examples and the face is perhaps a little more rounded in appearance, presenting a more stylized and traditional "portrait" type in the usual Egyptian fashion. All of these Egyptian statues representing Cleopatra VII as a ruler compare to the earlier representations of prominent royal women as the principal wife or daughter of the king of Egypt. In these statues Cleopatra appears as a very Egyptian queen, upholding the Egyptian royal tradition, but adding a twist in the development of iconography in the form of the triple cobras.

4.10 TEMPLES

In addition to considering the statues of Cleopatra VII it is necessary to investigate the temples that are associated with the queen. This particular body of evidence is important in any full assessment of Cleopatra and her rule, and yet any detailed discussions of material remains is often lacking. Many of these temples are fully published by IFAO and yet their wholly Egyptian appearance means that biographers of Cleopatra often ignore this evidence beyond mentioning the south wall of the temple of Hathor at Denderah. Cleopatra's dedications during the second half of her reign are discussed under the temple headings below.

Armant

Armant, also known as Hermonthis, is around a 20-minute drive from the modern tourist center of Luxor. In ancient terms this places the temple within a relatively close distance from the Theban temples of Karnak and Luxor. Situated on the West Bank of the Nile, today the modern village surrounds the walled ancient site. Many publications paint a bleak picture of preservation at the site; however, there are a number of relief decorations that are relevant to Cleopatra VII, and related to her father. As noted, the crypts of the main temple date to the reign of Ptolemy XII (Plates 3.3 and 3.6).

The birth house was built during the queen's rule with her son and there is evidence of her presence, in spite of this structure having been destroyed. Cleopatra's cartouche appears on the upper register of a relief (Plate 4.9). The cartouche is in the single form reading Cleopatra Father-loving in hieroglyphs (*nṯrt*

Plate 4.9 Architrave from the temple at Armant with the cartouche of Cleopatra (now stored upside down)

mr(t)-it.s (von Beckerath 1984: 294, E1). To the viewer's right of the name is the Horus falcon with outstretched wings protecting the cartouche. The inclusion of the Horus motif is consistently found for Cleopatra's male companion, her son Ptolemy XV, on the Denderah reliefs (see below) and perhaps suggests that the queen's status, or perhaps priorities, changed between the executions of the schemes of decoration at the two temples. Cleopatra's major contribution to the sanctuary at Armant was the birth house. The structure was recorded by early photographers and artists but was sadly demolished and its reliefs destroyed between 1861 and 1862. It was located behind the main temple (Arnold 1999: 222–4) and, like many of Cleopatra's projects, it is possible that it was started during the reign of her father. Cleopatra takes the title "the Female Horus" and is once called "the image of her father" (Tait 2003b: 4).

There have been attempts to reconstruct the building digitally (Arnold 1999: 222–3 figs. 179 and 180). It seems clear that the

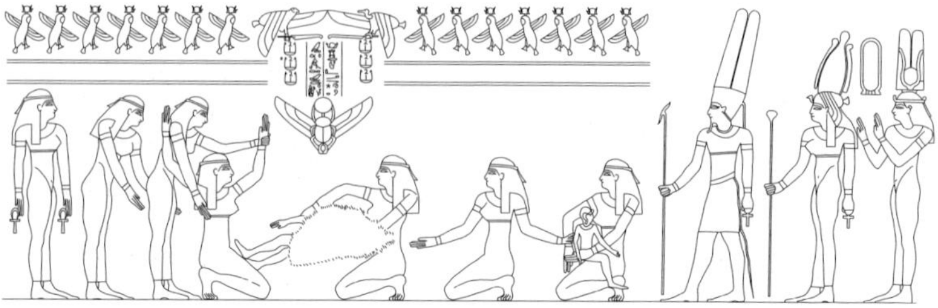

Figure 4.1 Drawing of the birth-scene in the Mammisi at Armant (after Lepsius)

main structure was surrounded by a colonnaded portico and that the sanctuary contained three rooms. Arnold has suggested that the building may have been built in three distinct phases: the main sanctuary being the first, a high entrance kiosk with four columns along the two sides and six at the front being added to the front of the early building, and then a second kiosk in front of this. This final stage had two columns at the sides and four at the front and was 16.55 meters high. The abaci (an abacus is the section above the column head) were deeper than usual and Arnold suggests that carved figures of Bes were intended to be added. An idea of how this might have looked can be gained from a comparison with the birth house at Edfu.

Within the sanctuary Lepsius recorded some truly remarkable relief decorations showing the birth of Horus the son (Lepsius 1849–59 vol. 4: pl. 60a). On the right, stand the gods Amun and Nekhbet; behind them Cleopatra VII raises her hands in prayer. She wears her usual crown of sun-disk and cow's horns and wears the royal cobra rather than divine vulture headdress. Her name intended within a single cartouche. Usually birth houses show Isis suckling the young Horus, but the Armant scene actually shows the birth of the child. Nurses hold the mother whilst others pull the child from her; another then passes the newborn baby to a nurse who is shown with him sitting on her knee. The parallel to Cleopatra and her son is obvious and above the child, as it is pulled from its mother's womb, is a

Plate 4.10 Relief decoration showing Cleopatra III, Deir el Medina

winged khepri beetle, which is linked to the son of Amun who is shown here. Elsewhere anthropomorphic bull-headed nurses suckle the child in a reference to the Buchis bull who lived at Armant. At the bottom of the scene Horus drinks directly from the udders of a cow. A more conventional scene accompanies that of the divine nurses – Isis suckles her son, who is adored (Lepsius 1849–59 vol. 4: pl. 59c).

Denderah

The original Temple of Hathor at Denderah dates to the New Kingdom and was enlarged by the Thirtieth Dynasty ruler Nectanebo I (Arnold 1999: 115). There were earlier Ptolemaic additions to buildings within the sanctuary during the reigns of Ptolemies VI, VIII, and IX. Plans to replace the main Hathor temple were made during the reign of Ptolemy XII and the main temple was dedicated on July 16 in year 27 of his rule, which equates to 54 BCE, four years before his death (Amer and Morardet 1983: 255; Cauville 1998: 5). The building work and decoration were undertaken during the reign of Cleopatra VII and for this reason the temple is an important source of information for the presentation of the queen, even when the cartouches remain blank, as is often the case on the internal walls. The building was completed by the Roman rulers Augustus, Tiberius, and possibly later during the reigns of Nero, Trajan, and Antoninus Pius (Devauchelle 1985: 174).[2]

Most publications on the subject of Cleopatra include an image of the south wall, which presents a well-known double scene showing Cleopatra and her son Ptolemy Caesar taking part in a ritual (Plate 4.11). A stela in the British Museum dates this decoration to the fifteenth year of her rule (Ray 2003: 10).

On the back wall of the temple Ptolemy XV presents an incense burner to the gods. He is identified as ruler of Upper and Lower Egypt by the two crowns placed upon a pair of ram's horns and two cobras. The headdress beneath the crown is called the "blue crown" and is associated with warfare. It is an interesting choice and appears elsewhere as one of the standard crowns worn by the young ruler. His kilt, which is worn with a longer ceremonial skirt, is decorated with a smiting scene. Such images were common on the pylons of temples (see Plate 3.7), and

Plate 4.11 The south wall of the Temple of Hathor at Denderah

represent the king attacking foreign captives. The cartouches on the kilt above the scene are blank. On the south wall at Denderah, Ptolemy XV is shown as the king of Egypt; he stands in the dominant position, in front of his mother, and is also protected by a Hawk, representing Horus, which flies above his head. His name, Ptolemy Caesar, is spelt out in the cartouches, accompanying his image. Cleopatra is shown as a royal figure taking part in a procession of offering; she holds a sistrum (rattle) in one of her hands and a *menat* necklace in the other (Bingen 2007: 73). She wears the crown associated with the majority of Ptolemaic queens consisting of a sun-disk and cow's horns with double plumes on a circlet of cobras for a base. On her brow is a cobra attached to a diadem and her wig is positioned behind her shoulders and falls onto her back. She is referred to as the "mistress of the two lands," a title that is repeated throughout the temple decoration whenever she appears. The cartouches elsewhere are mostly blank. In between the two rulers is the ka (spirit) of Ptolemy XV.

The same image appears on the right. Between Cleopatra and son is a smaller figure with an ankh and staff; the ka sign in the form of two raised hands identifies him as the ka (spirit) of Ptolemy Caesar. Opposite the rulers, the gods Ihy and his mother Hathor mimic the stance of Cleopatra and her son. As Ray has pointed out (2003: 9), Hathor was the perfect divine parallel for the queen because her consort, Horus, who appears on the relief after Hathor and her son, did not live within the same temple but was many miles away at Edfu. Ray has suggested that Cleopatra was naturally drawn to such a divine parallel (2003: 9–11). The other figures are from the Osirid triad stand in a line in front of the rulers. On the left, the rulers stand in front of gods that include Isis, her son Harsomteus, and Osiris (Ray 2003: 10).

Two dominant styles of decoration have been identified at Denderah (Bianchi 2003: 14–15). The so-called festive style is epitomized by the colossal scene on the rear wall of the temple. Here, there is an attention to detail that is not found on the inside of the temple (Bianchi 2003: 14). The second style inside the temple is lacking in detail, as seen from the many blank cartouches and also the style of carving. The proportions of features such as arms and hands of the figures on the inside walls and crypts are often incorrect (see Bianchi 2003: pl. 1b). There is also less careful attention to filling the spaces around the figures or perhaps, more correctly, if the figures were carved after the text (Bianchi 2003: 15), the carving of the figurative decoration was standardized rather than prescriptive.

Inside the temple a survey of the relief decoration shows that nearly all of the Ptolemaic cartouches are blank. Images of a lone male king prevail and occasionally a consort joins him. Her names are also missing, but she is awarded the title "Ruler and Mistress of the Two Lands." There is usually one blank cartouche, but on some occasions there are two. She rarely appears alone and always takes the secondary position allowing her consort to stand directly in front of the gods. She mostly holds an ankh sign in one hand and raises her other in prayer. On occasion she presents offerings. The reliefs and their inscriptions have been published by Cauville (1998, 1999, 2000a, 2000b, 2001, and 2004a and b). Below there follow references to images of Cleopatra VII from inside the temple. I am suggesting below that the images of a nameless royal female accompanying a male ruler, who stands in front of her in all of the offering scenes, is that of Cleopatra VII and her son Ptolemy XV. These representations appear inside the main temple, on the inner and outer walls of chapels. This particular phase of decoration would have been undertaken well into the programme of works; the crypts, amongst the first, are decorated with images of Cleopatra VII (Bianchi 2003). Ptolemy XII only lived for three further years after the dedication of Denderah, and its seems that his daughter continued the project. Following Cleopatra's death Augustus was swift to make his own mark at the site. Fortunately for the present purposes of writing on the dedications by Cleopatra VII, the emperor's agents left her work both in and outside the temple.

In room D, west wall, lower register (Cauville 2000: vol. 1, 14 and vol. 2, pl 15 top and 27), Cleopatra appears behind her consort; he wears the crown of Upper and Lower Egypt and presents a necklace to Hathor. Cleopatra stands with one arm raised in prayer and the other by her side, in which she clutches an ankh sign. Her crown is the standard type worn by Ptolemaic queens, as on the back wall of the temple, in the form of a sun-disk, cow's horns, and double plumes. There is a single blank cartouche with the title "ruler, mistress of the two lands" above her image, and the male ruler has two blank cartouches. In the southern corner of room E Cleopatra appears again (Cauville 2000: vol. 1, 62 and vol. 2, pl. 40 lower) in the same form and with the same titles. On the lower register of the east wall the queen holds an offering table mimicking her consort (Cauville 2000: vol. 2, pl. 45), and appears on the lower register of the north wall with the title "mistress of the two lands" (Cauville 2000: vol. 1, 71). In room F west wall on the lower register Cleopatra offers two wine jars (Cauville 2000: vol. 2, pl. 97).

On the outer columns of the south wall of the exterior of the sanctuary (Cauville 1998: pl. 7) Cleopatra appears with her consort; elsewhere the male ruler stands alone. The queen wears her usual costume and crown and is shown with one hand raised in prayer, the other holding an ankh. Details (Cauville 1998: pl. xlix, lvii, and lxxvi, lxxxiv) illustrate the uniformity of her representation. The titles are the usual ones of this ruler: "mistress of the two lands" (Cauville 1998: 168–9, 176–7, 200, and 208–10).

Cleopatra also joins her consort on the interior, central, vestibule gate holding wine jars, on the east wall of the "robe" room on the lowest register with an ankh sign and one hand raised, on the treasury door with the usual stance and attire but with two black cartouches, and in the Upper Hathor chapel (Cauville 2001: pls. i–ii, iii, xii, xiv, xxiv, and xxvi respectively). It is probably significant that both a single (Cauville 2001: pl. xcviii and pl. cxiv) and a double cartouche (Cauville 2001: pl. cxix) are used. The titles (Cauville 2001: 210–11, 137–9, and 244–7) are the usual ones of the ruler: "mistress of the two lands." Where there are two cartouches the two titles are split. Double blank cartouches can also be found in the west wall room, south-east second register from the top (vol 3, 38–43, lines 4–5, pl. i and pl. ii, lines 5–6). In one scene Cleopatra stands with one hand raised in prayer behind her consort who presents a bennu bird to Hathor (Cauville 2000a: pl. 1). Cleopatra is also accompanied by her usual titles and two blank cartouches (Cauville 2000: 34–9).

One of the early drawings of the north wall shows two fragments of reliefs with images of Cleopatra back to back, presumably behind her consort, who is now missing (Cauville 2004: pl. viii). In the southern crypt room A north wall Cleopatra appears with her usual dress and in her usual stance with two blank cartouches, and in the western crypt no. 3 she is shown with her consort with both hands raised in prayer and with an inscribed cartouche (Cauville 2004a: pl. lx). The single cartouche reappears on the west wall of the same crypt (west 3) and the stance is back to that of one arm raised, the other hand holding an ankh. The titles are the usual ones of the ruler: "mistress of the two lands" (Cauville 2004a: 462–3).

On the corridor walls there is a notable change in one of the offering scenes featuring the Cleopatra (Cauville 1999: pls. v, x), which show the queen in her usual dress and stance (Plates 4.9, 4.11 and 4.12) with a single cartouche, but in one particular scene she wears the crown of Arsinoe II (Plate 4.13). In one particularly important scene on the lower register of room 4 east, west wall (Cauville 1999: pl. xvi), Cleopatra appears alone, without Ptolemy Caesar. This is the only example that I have been able to find on the temple walls or in Cauville's publications. Cleopatra has one blank cartouche and stands behind a personification of Lower Egypt and the god of the inundation, Hapi, who holds the papyrus of the Delta. In the center of the scene is a depiction of Horus in the form of a hawk on an offering table. On the right side of the scene and the other side of the offering table is her consort, wearing the dual crown of Upper and Lower Egypt, standing behind a personification of Upper Egypt and Hapi with the lotus of the South.

Plate 4.12 Ptolemy XV Caesar and Cleopatra VII making an offering, Temple of Hathor at Denderah. Cleopatra wears the generic form of crown

Plate 4.13 Ptolemy XV Caesar and Cleopatra making an offering, Temple of Hathor at Denderah. Cleopatra wears the crown of Arsinoe II

Ptolemy XV is often accompanied by gods in the offering scenes, which may explain why he is alone. The overall message of the internal relief decoration at Denderah is that Ptolemy XV is the ruler and he typically takes part in the rituals and offerings without his mother. The blank cartouches are symptomatic of the instability of the later Ptolemaic period. Cleopatra is named in only a handful of instances (Cauville 2004b: 555). The single version of the cartouche appears on one occasion in the small Hathor chapel (Plate 4.14a) where she is named simply as "Cleopatra." However, elsewhere in the part of the building the queen appears with the more usual blank cartouches (Plate 4.14b).

The roof chapels of the temple have also been attributed to Cleopatra (Cauville 1997: 76–7). The chapels were designed for the eclipse of March 7, 51 BCE, and were dedicated on December 28, 47 BCE, thus demonstrating the close ties between Ptolemy XII's designs and his daughter's completion of his projects.

Kalabsha

In his 2003 essay for the *Cleopatra Reassessed* conference volume, Bianchi drew attention to two further reliefs he believes represent Cleopatra VII. The first is something of a ghost in that the text records a dedication by Cleopatra but the figurative frieze and titles show the image and names of Augustus. The text appears on a gateway from the temple at Kalabsha (Bianchi 2003: 15) and is now housed in the Berlin Egyptian Museum. There is room on the relief for two figures but only one appears: an image of Augustus, occupies the space. The space suggests that the reliefs were carved during the Ptolemaic period, and the inscription referring to the Cleopatra confirms the identity of the original rulers as Cleopatra with one of her male consorts (Bianchi 2003: 15). If this relief was re-carved with the image of Augustus as the evidence suggests, this act is distinct to the more usual policy of placing his image close to that of the queen, as at Denderah and Koptos.

Plate 4.14a Chapel of Hathor at Denderah

Other relief fragments

A relief fragment now in a private collection contains an inscription that suggests the missing royal figure was female (Bianchi 2003: 15). The cartouche is of a form found in the crypts of the Armant temple, which date to the reign of Ptolemy XII. They read "great house" (the name used for pharaoh). Cleopatra VII

Plate 4.14b Cartouche reading "Cleopatra" from the Hathor Chapel Denderah

was the only Ptolemaic queen to stand alone on temple relief representations and as this brief survey has shown, following the succession of her son Ptolemy XV Caesar, Cleopatra more commonly appeared with her consort.

4.11 HELLENISTIC QUEEN

There is little to suggest that Cleopatra wished to be seen as a Hellenistic monarch in Egypt. The only exception to this observation is the representation of Cleopatra on coinage and on a small number of fragments of marble, Greek-style statues in the form of portraits that have been associated with the queen. Since coinage was not traditionally used in Egypt, I assume that this medium was aimed at an international audience or perhaps the armies who protected the queen and her country. Cleopatra's continuation of the cult title "father-loving" is one example of a non-Egyptian aspect, but the ruler cults had been adopted enthusiastically by the Egyptian priesthood and temples during the reign of Ptolemy II, and so had been a part of the native religious tradition for over 200 years. Nevertheless, here we find a continuation of an essentially Greek concept. Although there has been much debate over the origins of the Ptolemaic royal and dynastic cults, the fact that contemporary Hellenistic rulers subscribed to the same titles as their Ptolemaic counterparts would suggest that the idea had been inherited from the Macedonian court, or inspired by Alexander.

Amongst the papers of the 2003 British Museum conference *Cleopatra Reassessed* (Walker and Ashton 2003) a number of new possible "portraits" of Cleopatra in the Hellenistic Greek style were identified. It is important to stress that these portraits are probably no closer to Cleopatra's true appearance than the Egyptian-style representations. Art historians tend to label such images "naturalistic," a term that is misleading and that is also bound within European cultural assumptions. The first Greek-style "portrait" (Walker and Higgs 2003: 71–4) is smaller than other recognized Greek-style representations, measuring only 23 centimeters in height, and has a particularly long neck, suggesting that it was once slotted into a body, probably of a different material. The Egyptian provenance is uncertain. The head was initially in the collections of the Musée Guimet and is now housed in the Louvre. The characteristic snail-shell curls that appear on the forehead are more stylized than those of other Greek-style representations that have been identified as the queen. This particular feature was first seen in a stylized archaizing form of the portraits of Cleopatra II and Cleopatra III and was replicated on some of the Egyptian-style statues that have been identified as Cleopatra VII (Ashton 2001a: 47). The hair of the Louvre head seems to have been styled in a melon coiffure and the queen appears to have worn a diadem, a feature that is not found in the queen's Egyptian-style representations. On the Egyptian statues a corkscrew hairstyle is coupled with the stylized curls that form a fringe. The portrait is not as youthful as the examples from Rome or another representing either Cleopatra VII or her daughter Cleopatra Selene in Cherchel, Algeria (Walker and Higgs 2003: 72).

The head in question seems to represent a mature woman and this, along with stylistic analysis, has led some scholars to suggest that the image was posthumous (Kyrieleis 1975: 86). This suggestion is unlikely since Cleopatra appears to represent a living royal queen rather than a goddess. If it does represent this particular queen the head is likely to date to her lifetime, and may show an alternative to the youthful representations that were manufactured in Rome (Plates 3.12 and 3.13). The statue has also been dated to the reign of Cleopatra Selene on account of the stylized snail-shell curls, which find parallels on the mummy portraits of the first century CE but, as noted, this feature can be found on images from the time of Cleopatra II, Cleopatra III, and Cleopatra VII. The essential difference between the Louvre head and the images of Cleopatra II and Cleopatra III is that its features are mature but feminine; there is no reference to the representations of a masculine appearance that were found on images of Cleopatra III in particular (Plate 4.5). In fact the Greek-style representations of Cleopatra VII seem to have been a deliberate attempt to return to the ideals of the early third century BC (Ashton 2003a: 95). Cleopatra's "portraits" are a hybrid of queens Arsinoe II, Berenice II, and Arsinoe III and share some features with those of her father, most notably the nose and prominent chin. The fuller face is similar to that of Berenice II (Ashton 2003a: 80–5), overall the mature quality of the Louvre head is not dissimilar to that of Arsinoe III, and yet, on the Greek-style heads found in Italy, there is youthful characteristic that copies the portrait type of Arsinoe II, her role model (compare Ashton 2003a: 76–9).

Another marble head in a private collection of more usual under-life-size proportions has also been linked to the youthful Cleopatra (Bianchi 2003: 20, pl. 6). Like the Louvre head, this example has a long slender neck, suggestive of the usual Ptolemaic classical tradition of slotting a portrait into a body of another material. The hair seems to be unfinished rather than the surface worn, in accordance with the Alexandrian technique of completing marble sculpture with a layer of stucco (plaster). A broad diadem is just discernible, marking the statue as a royal representation. The "portrait" is convincing as an image of Cleopatra VII; the mouth is sullen in appearance, the chin is well defined and the overall shape of the face is rounded with a straight nose and low forehead. The features have been compared to those on the coins minted in Damascus in 37/36 BCE (Bianchi 2003: n. 105), suggesting that the image is an early one. The youthful appearance supports this hypothesis.

Bianchi also draws attention to a second Greek-style "portrait" also in a private collection (2003: 19, pl. 5). This image represents a more mature woman with harsher features. The eyes are deeply set, the mouth is down-turned in the usual fashion but the lips are thinner, forcing a crease at the corners of the mouth. The cheekbones are higher and the chin is prominent and pointed in profile. The portrait is very similar to the well-known Vatican Cleopatra, which was manufactured in Italy (Plate 3.12). The head is broken at the neck and so it is not possible to determine if this section was slotted into a body or whether it was part of a whole statue. It has been suggested that the head was produced in Alexandria on account of the unfinished hair on the crown of the head, which is roughly carved and so, it is assumed, was finished in stucco as part of the usual manufacturing process. The hair that frames the face has been carved, as has a large *nodus* (knot) on top of the head. This particular feature appears in a much smaller form on both the Berlin and Vatican heads of Cleopatra (Walker 2003b), and it has been suggested that Cleopatra adopted this style at a key point during her reign. The attribute was clearly part of the artistic repertoire employed during her stay in Rome, as indicated on the aforementioned heads. The newly identified portrait has a confusing feature which appears to be a plait of hair but which may be a diadem, running under the *nodus* (knot) and the unfinished bun at the back of the head. Unlike the usual diadem this feature here is narrow, perhaps suggesting that a broader, more usual form of diadem was added above, either in stucco or gold.

4.12 COINAGE

The Alexandrian coinage presents further reference to Cleopatra VII's status as a Hellenistic queen. It is noteworthy that the queen appears alone on the coinage minted in Egypt rather than using the medium as a means of promoting her son. Her image is reminiscent of that of her father: strong jaw line, down-turned mouth, large eye (a reference to Herakles that began early in the Dynasty), and a strong, slightly hooked nose. I do not wish to discuss here the question of Cleopatra's beauty; it seems pointless and irrelevant whether the queen was attractive to the modern viewer. I prefer to describe her image as powerful and with clear reference to the representation of her father, and to note the important connection between the two.

The only coins to be produced were in copper alloy and silver. The gold coins of the early Ptolemaic period had long ceased to be produced (Walker and Higgs 2001: 177). Silver coins were also debased to 40 percent silver, compared to 80–90 percent during Ptolemy XII's rule and 98–99 percent of silver in the tetradrachms of the early Ptolemies (Hazzard 2000: 89–107). Silver drachms were minted in years 6 and 11 of Cleopatra's rule, 47/46 and 42/41 BCE respectively (Walker and Higgs 2001: 177, no. 178). The image on the obverse shows the queen wearing a royal diadem and with the characteristic small curls of hair around her forehead and at the nape of her neck. On the reverse is the Ptolemaic eagle and the legend reading "Cleopatra Queen."

Bronze coins were the most commonly minted during Cleopatra's reign. Although the production of bronze coinage had declined during the reigns of her immediate predecessors, Cleopatra once again started large scale production in this metal (Walker and Higgs 2001: 177–8). It is not possible to date most of these coins to a specific year. Coins were valued by a mark (a Greek *pi* or *mu*) rather than weight, as had been traditionally the case (Walker and Higgs 2001: 178, no. 183–5). This decision, along with the debasement of the silver coins, indicates a very deliberate policy to control the Alexandrian mint; its consequences will be explored further in chapter 7, below. It may be possible to place the coins into groups and then perhaps a relative sequence through the development of the "portrait" type of Cleopatra on the obverse, with the more exaggerated images towards the period when the queen minted coins with images of herself and Mark Antony. A comparison of the examples cited in Walker and Higgs (2001: 177 no. 180–2) suggests that there was a development over her 21-year rule. There are two distinct portrait types to emerge from the Alexandrian mint (Walker 2003b: 508–9): one shows an idealized portrait (Walker 2003b: fig. 1a), the other is closer to the representations of Cleopatra's predecessors and especially her father (Walker 2003b: fig. 1b). Both forms show the queen as a ruler as indicated by the royal diadem rather than the divine crown. It has, however, been suggested that this type of image, often referred to as "realistic" because of the prominent nose and chin, was intended as a gesture to Julius Caesar and emulates the Roman Republican form of portraiture (Spaer 1999: 347–50; Walker 2003b: 508–9). Neither form of image was exclusive to Alexandria; overseas examples have greatly aided an understanding of its chronological development.

4.13 REGENT

Ptolemy XV is barely mentioned in the Roman sources. There are several references to Cleopatra's relationship with Julius Caesar in Lucan's *Pharsalia* (63–109), including the birth of their child "a brother to Julia" (90). Plutarch's *Julius Caesar* (chapter 49) states that Caesar left Cleopatra on the throne following the Alexandrian wars, and went to Syria. The author states that when Julius Caesar left Egypt in 37 BCE Cleopatra was in her seventh month of pregnancy (Caesar 49.10), and that "a little later she had a son by him whom the Alexandrians called Caesarion" (Jones 2006: 58). That Ptolemy XV was Caesar's son is mentioned by Plutarch during his account of the Donations of Alexandria (*Life of Antony*, ch. 54; Jones 2006: 116), and in reference to his fate around the time of Cleopatra's suicide (Jones 2006: 187).

Suetonius (*Divine Julius Caesar*, chapter 52) wrote that Cleopatra was allowed to call her son by Caesar his name (Jones 2006:

79). The writer goes on to comment that "several Greek writers record that he was like Caesar in both appearance and bearing." Mark Antony confirmed to the Senate that Caesar had actually acknowledged the child, yet one of Caesar's friends, Gaius Oppius, was said later to have published a book stating that Ptolemy Caesar was not Caesar's son (Edwards 2000). The fate of Ptolemy XV will be considered further in chapter 9 (below).

Following her return from Rome in 44 BCE, Cleopatra wasted no time in dispatching her younger brother and taking Ptolemy Caesar as her co-ruler and yet it is only later in her reign that there is evidence for her son's role as ruler of Egypt. The date of Ptolemy Caesar's birth is disputed. It was thought for many years that Cleopatra's first child was born in 46 BCE following Julius Caesar's initial visit to Egypt, and that he was conceived during the time it took Caesar to ensure the security of the state of the country. The secure dating was on account of a demotic stela from the Sarapieion at Memphis that is now in the Louvre Museum. The stela dates to a birthday that was read as that of Ptolemy Caesar's in June 23, 47 BCE (Hölbl 2001: 238). An important article in 2001, however, indicated that the date name, thought to be Caesar, and so Ptolemy Caesar, was not a correct reading (Devauchelle 2001).

Of the other children by Mark Antony, of whom there were three – the twins Cleopatra Selen and Alexander Helios, and then Ptolemy Philadelphos – there are some references. In the *Deified Augustus* (17) Suetonius claims that Mark Antony named his children with Cleopatra as his heirs and for this, his "abandonment of the ways of a Roman citizen," he was declared an enemy of the state. In chapter 6 of his *History*, Dio describes preparations by Antony and Cleopatra to assert their childrens' positions; not only was Ptolemy Caesar mentioned but also Antyllus, Antony's son by Fulvia. Dio states that the two rulers did this to "arouse the enthusiasm of the Egyptians, who would feel that they had at last a man for their king, and to cause the rest to continue the struggle with these boys as their leaders, in case anything untoward should happen to the parents." The historian then points out that this act was the downfall of the two boys, who were seen to be a threat by Octavian and so put to death upon capture.

The young prince took the titles "the god who loves his mother" and "the god who loves his father" (Bingen 2007: 64). During Cleopatra's sixteenth regnal year, 37/36 BCE, the queen started a system of double dating, calling this year 1 to coincide with the Donations of Alexandria (Bingen 2007: 57).

4.14 STATUES OF PTOLEMY XV

There are two groups of statues that have been associated with Ptolemy XV. The first are Egyptian in style and borrow Greek-style features in the established Ptolemaic tradition. Statues within this group are supported by the usual back pillar and are carved from a hard stone. The second group belong to the Greek tradition. They are made from stones used for Egyptian statuary – granite, steatite, or limestone – but are in a Greek form of a tapering rectangular base, often with a phallus and attachments at the shoulders. This type of statue is known as a herm because early examples often had the head of the god Hermes surmounting the plinth and were originally used to mark roads. The proposed examples with the head of Ptolemy Caesar have Greek-style features and iconography.

Statues in both groups have the "portrait" features or iconographic attributes to suggest that they represent a young prince. They all share facial features that are similar to those on statues that have been identified as belonging to Cleopatra VII (Ashton 2003d: 26–30). The statues of Ptolemy Caesar conform to a type that is now referred to as bi-lingual. This is because the necessary attributes are present to identify the statue as a king of Egypt for the Egyptian audience but, in addition, the facial features reproduce a recognizable (but not necessarily realistic) portrait according to an accepted Greek type. The statues, therefore, provide us with examples of Ptolemy XV's presentation to the Greeks. His images served both cultures and also provided an important subliminal message regarding his affinity to Egypt. Rome might have rejected him as the rightful heir of Julius Caesar, but Egypt welcomed the young ruler alongside his mother and as his mother's rightful heir.

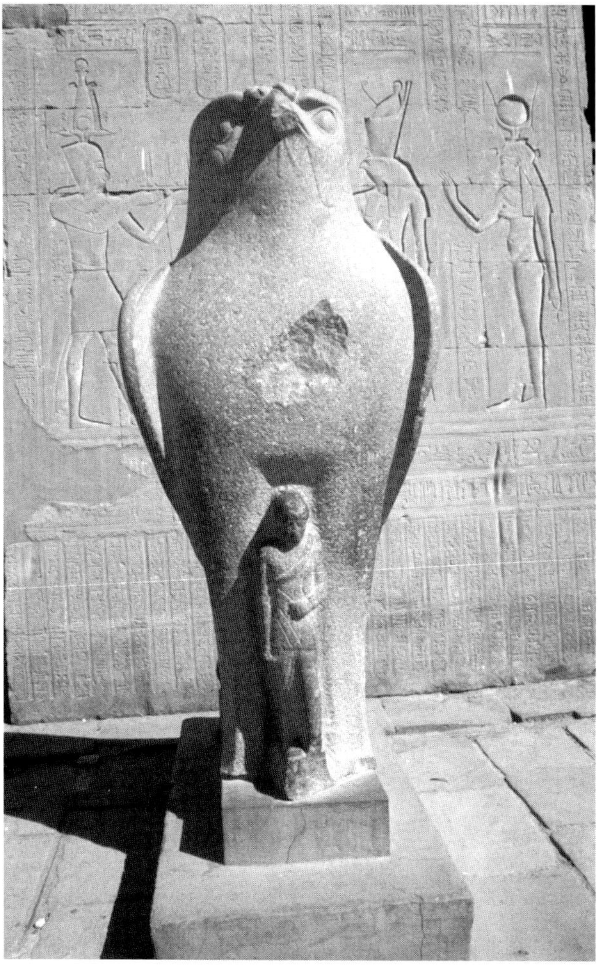

Plate 4.15 Statue of Horus with the young Ptolemy XV Caesar as a priest. Temple of Horus at Edfu

A statue that falls between the two categories under discussion here is the representation of Ptolemy Caesar as a priest at the temple of Horus at Edfu (Plate 4.15). A large Horus falcon stands over a small figure, thought to represent Cleopatra's son as a prince (Weil Goudchaux 2001: 138–9). The idea of a falcon standing over the ruler in protective role is a long established one. There is a statue of smaller scale but the closest in date to the proposed representation of Ptolemy XV is now housed in the Metropolitan Museum, New York and dates to the Thirtieth Dynasty.

As with all Ptolemaic sculptures, there is some debate over the identification of the representations of Ptolemy XV. There are six possible candidates for group one, Egyptian statues with Greek-style "portrait" features. The most complete example is unprovenanced and now housed in the Brooklyn Museum of Art (Ashton 2001a: 30–2, 96–7, no. 30; Stanwick 2002: 61, 125, E16). All publications of this piece conclude that it was manufactured in the first century BCE. The statue is Egyptian, it has a back pillar and the stance is the usual one with the left leg striding forwards (Plate 4.16). The legs and base are missing. The

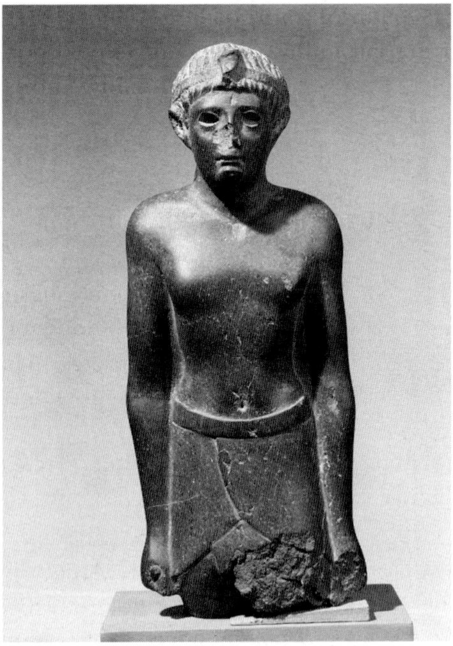

Plate 4.16 Basalt statue of Ptolemy Caesar. Brooklyn Museum of Art, Brooklyn, inv. 54.117

preserved section measures 30 centimeters and so the piece would have been comparable in size to the Hermitage and San Jose statues attributed to Cleopatra VII (Plates 4.6 and 4.8, pp. 83–7). The prince wears a flat diadem (a feature of Greek and Egyptian art) and a single cobra attached to the front. The hair is short and combed forwards. The square, prominent chin and down turned mouth are typical of the images associated with his mother. A similar head from a statue is now housed in the National Museum in Warsaw (Ashton 2001a: 96–7, no. 30). In this representation the ruler wears only a diadem and is without a uraeus, thus suggesting that the model was a Greek-style representation. The attribution of this particular piece to Ptolemy Caesar is less certain in the literature; however, the features seem to correspond well to the aforementioned Brooklyn statue.

There are three further statues that may represent Ptolemy Caesar; all have a provenance and all are Egyptian in style (striding stance, back pillar, kilt and *nemes* headcloth – a headdress worn by male rulers and some gods). The first is questionable. It is said to have come from Karnak and is now in the Egyptian Museum in Cairo and measures 96 centimeters in height (Ashton 2001a: 98–9, no. 33; Stanwick 2002: 38, 119–20, D14, dating the piece to the reigns of Ptolemies IX–X). The portrait features are similar to those discussed above, but the styling of the hair beneath the *nemes* headcloth is different and some have suggested more likely to be early Roman in date. There is another important feature missing from this essentially Egyptian statue – the uraeus on the brow. There are two examples of Egyptian statues, early Roman in date, that also lack a royal cobra (Kiss 1984: 142, fig. 78 and 147, figs. 96–7).

The identity of the second example from this group is controversial, but specialists generally agree that it dates to the reign of Cleopatra VII (Plate 4.17). The question is whether it represents Ptolemy XII, Ptolemy XV Caesar or Mark Antony (Ashton 2003d; Stanwick 2002: 18, E1, and E2; Ashton 2006: review of Stanwick: 548). The latter is extremely unlikely since the Romans did not adopt the role of pharaoh and, like the Cairo statue, this piece shows a ruler with a *nemes* headcloth, but also with the

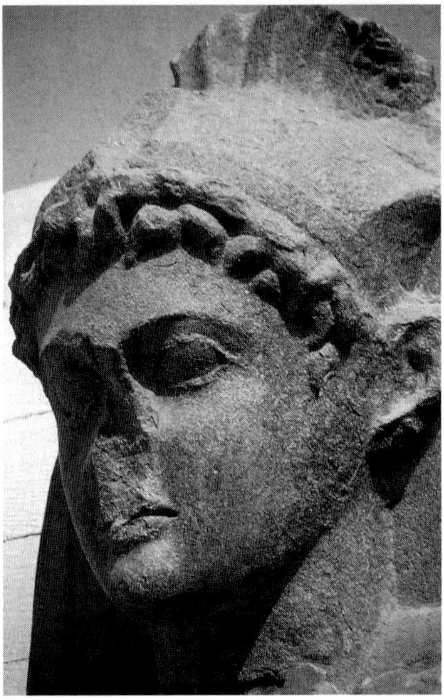

Plate 4.17 Granite statue of Ptolemy Caesar. Greco-Roman Museum, Alexandria, inv. 11275

usual uraeus. The statue was found in eastern Alexandria and is now housed in the Greco-Roman Museum there. It is part of a dyad that included a statue of Cleopatra VII as Isis (Plate 4.18) from a site that is discussed in chapter 6 below. The statue has youthful features that correspond to those on other statues of Ptolemy XV. Drawings from the time of the discovery indicate that he wore an Egyptian *hm.hmt* crown. This particular attribute was associated with rulers and with the god Harpocrates and so would be a logical choice to use on a representation of Ptolemy XV as the son of Cleopatra as Isis. As with other representations where the pair appear together, they are shown as equals. Here on the Alexandrian statue Cleopatra is a goddess and her son is ruler of Egypt.

Plate 4.18 Granite statue of Cleopatra VII as Isis. Copyright © the Royal Museum of Mariemont

The third statue is the most recent to have been discovered and, like the dyad, it was found in Alexandria. The statue was originally published as a representation of Augustus as pharaoh of Egypt. However, it was subsequently suggested that the portrait type was similar to that of Cleopatra VII and that the youthful image represented her son, Ptolemy XV (Ashton 2003d: 29–30). This statue is unique in that it has a feature not found on any other Ptolemaic, or indeed Pharaonic, statue: two holes beneath the folds of the *nemes* head cloth. This element clearly allowed for the attachment of an additional attribute; it has been suggested that this was the horns of Amun and that in this way Ptolemy XV was linked to the golden age of the Ptolemaic dynasty by linking himself with Alexander, who was believed to be the son of the god.

A substantial group and significant number of statues in the form of a Greek "Herm" may also be associated with Ptolemy Caesar. The statues are now housed in the following museums: the Civic Museum Bologna (Ashton 2001a: 98–9, no. 32); Brooklyn (Ashton 2001a: 68, 3.1); the Petrie Museum London (Ashton 2001a: 68, no. 3.2); the Fitzwilliam Museum Cambridge (Ashton 2004: 20–1, no. 6); and Cairo (unpublished). All examples have hair styled in the same manner as the Warsaw head and the Brooklyn statue. Their portrait features are similar but not identical, suggesting that they do not form part of a group from a single workshop. They are all around the same proportions, measuring 10 centimeters to include the shoulders, with the exception of the Cairo example, which is substantially larger. It seems likely that they performed a cult purpose, either within sanctuaries or personal shrines. Sadly, none has an exact provenance. They all have a distinctive feature in the form of a twisted diadem, the meaning of which is uncertain. They are important because they suggest mass production of a specific form of statue of the young ruler. Such images are common, in the form of Greek-style portrait heads, during the third century BCE (Ashton 2001a: 9), but then cease to be produced in the same numbers. The re-emergence of royal portraits for cult purposes suggests a renaissance during the late Ptolemaic period.

NOTES

1 I am extremely grateful to Willy Clarysse for allowing me to see a pre-publication copy of this article.
2 I would like to thank R. S. Bianchi for our numerous discussions on this subject and for his advice on bibliographic references.

5

CLEOPATRA'S CAPITAL AND COURT

5.1 ALEXANDRIA AS THE PTOLEMAIC CAPITAL

According to Diodorus writing c. 59 BCE Alexandria had 300,000 free inhabitants implying a total population of around 500,000 (Rowlandson 2003: 253). The Alexandrians, a formidable force throughout the Ptolemaic period, often intervened if they felt their rightful ruler was in danger. In 131 BCE they selected Cleopatra II to rule in place of her husband and brother Ptolemy VIII and his new second wife, her daughter, Cleopatra III. When later Cleopatra III wanted to replace her son Ptolemy IX as her co-ruler she used the Alexandrians to carry out her will. The queen cleverly fabricated a story in which her son had threatened her life, and had some of her guards beaten in order to substantiate the tale. The mob obliged and the king was exiled (Ashton 2003a: 65–6). When Cleopatra Berenice was murdered by Ptolemy XI, less than three weeks after their marriage, the assailant was executed in the stadium by the Alexandrians (Ashton 2003a: 66–7). Even during the reign of Cleopatra VII the residents of the capital city played an integral role in the power struggle between sibling rulers. These are just a handful of examples to illustrate the power of the people of Alexandria.

Alexandria was the administrative capital as well as the royal residence for most of the Ptolemaic period. The city is often seen to be the cultural capital of Egypt, but this is only true for Greek culture. The royal house had funded an institution which was called the Mouseion, or shrine of the Muses, and from which we take the word museum. The Ptolemaic Mouseion was more akin to a private research center whose aim was to glorify its patrons. Manetho, one of the few Egyptians to have been patronized by the Ptolemaic royal house, is often cited as an example of the early rulers' desire to promote the native culture (Fraser 1972: 505–11). Modern classical scholars often seem to forget that for this one center of Greek culture there were hundreds of Egyptian temples developing and promoting Egyptian culture, language, and scholarship. The golden age for the Mouseion was the third century BCE. Scholars often cite political problems, both internal and external, as the reason for the collapse of this scholarly institution.

A study of the surviving archaeology and material evidence for Ptolemaic patronage throughout the period has, however, shown that in Egypt, the rulers' interests shift towards their presentation as Egyptian pharaoh rather than Hellenistic king (Ashton 2003b: 213–24). Whether or not the rulers genuinely preferred their Egyptian identity or whether this move was mainly to win the support of the Egyptian priesthood is difficult to assess. Given the flamboyant characters of many second-century rulers, it is easier to see why the rulers chose to present themselves as Egyptian rather than Greek kings. Their attitude to taxation was, however, quite different and the Ptolemies functioned within a monetized economy. The rulers followed a policy of progressively removing the financial autonomy of the temples. Allowances were given but the temples were dependent upon royal gestures.

The Egyptian priests were an indigenous equivalent to the Greeks of Alexandria. In the context of Egyptian religion the priests legitimized Ptolemaic rule and offered ways in which the rulers could be promoted. Hölbl (2001: 280–9) suggests that how well the relationship between ruler and priesthoods functioned was dependent on both being willing to play their necessary roles. The priests, however, needed a king (admittedly not necessarily a Ptolemy); without a ruler the Egyptian cosmos could not function. Temples were also dependent on the royal house for a good deal of their revenue, either through tax concessions or through funding new building works and cults, which equaled jobs. Just as the Greek administration obtained favors from the king (Samuel 1993: 179), so did the Egyptian priesthood. Rulers regularly visited temples; according to the dedication text at the temple of Horus at Edfu, Ptolemy VIII and Cleopatra II actually visited the site (Hölbl 2001: 280).

The dedications made by the first four rulers at Alexandria and Memphis show a willingness and awareness by the rulers of the need to promote the mutual acculturation of Greek and Egyptian cultures. In Alexandria the rulers established a Greek temple to Egyptian gods Osiris and Apis as the amalgam Osarapis, which was the cult object of the dead Apis bull at Memphis. The Greek version of the god was awarded a Greek-style cult statue and was closely associated with the royal house (Ashton 2004a: 21–5). At Memphis, which was the royal residence for the early part of Ptolemy I's reign, the rulers maintained a close relationship with the priesthood and many were crowned there. In the early Ptolemaic period the rulers dedicated a sculptural monument in the style of a Hellenistic victory monument at the site (Ashton 2003c: 10–14). At first glance the Greek-style representations of philosophers, playwrights, and poets seem an incongruous and insensitive addition to a traditional Egyptian sanctuary. It has, however, been suggested that the figures represented Greek scholars who had themselves spent time in Egypt, thus legitimizing the position of the new Greek rulers within Egypt's history.

5.2 CLEOPATRA'S ALEXANDRIA AS CAPITAL CITY: ARCHAEOLOGICAL REMAINS

Alexandria during the reign of Cleopatra VII was very different to the city of the early Ptolemaic rulers. According to the geographer Strabo, who visited the city just after the death of Cleopatra, the boundaries had expanded eastwards. The extent of this growth is rarely fully comprehended by modern scholars. The temple of Isis, which dates to the reign of Cleopatra, must have been positioned in a prime location. Its construction must have been by far the largest building programme during the queen's

Plate 5.1 Marble statue of Cleopatra VII as Isis, found at the sanctuary of Isis in Rome. Archivio Fotografico dei Musei Capitolini

rule and, unlike many other temples further south, the Alexandrian temple of Isis seems to have been begun during her reign and to have continued in use during the Roman period. The two surviving busts from the colossal dyad of Cleopatra and her son, which were dedicated at the site, are testimony to the scale of the complex. The statue of Cleopatra as Isis is one of the most remarkable to survive from her rule (Plate 4.17). This sanctuary was vastly different to the temple dedicated to Julius Caesar, the Caesareum, which was located close to the old center of the Ptolemaic capital.

The temple to Julius Caesar was begun by Cleopatra VII but was unfinished at the time of her death. Augustus, as Caesar's chosen heir was naturally keen to complete the project. Thanks to a detailed description of the temple in the mid-first century BCE and excavations at the site in 1992–3, we know a reasonable amount about the developed form of this sanctuary (Empereur 2002: 112–23). Prior to Augustus' building, the temple dedicated to the Deified Julius Caesar included a shrine or altar dedicated to Mark Antony (Empereur 2002: 112). Philo of Alexandria described the Roman temple as follows: "For there is elsewhere no precinct like that which is called the Sebasteum, a temple to Caesar (Augustus), patron of sailors, positioned on a prominence facing the harbours . . . consisting of a huge precinct, embellished with porticoes, libraries, men's banqueting halls, groves, propylaea, spacious courts, open-air rooms." Augustus also brought two obelisks from Heliopolis, an abandoned temple that is close to modern Cairo's airport (Habachi 1987: 152–82), known today as Cleopatra's needles. The obelisks, which date to the reign of Thutmose III, are today on the bank of the Thames in London and in Central Park, New York.

Excavations (Empereur 2002: 115–17) indicate that the temple still functioned as a sanctuary dedicated to the Imperial cult at the end of the second century CE. In the fourth century CE the temple became the site of a Christian cathedral (Empereur 2002: 116–17). This vast site may still yield further information as and when buildings around this region of the city are demolished and developed.

Strabo mentioned that the royal palaces were positioned along the seafront, presumably because this was the best location in the city, particularly given Alexandria's humid summers. The position of the modern corniche, as the seafront is now called, bears little relationship to that during the Ptolemaic period. The Ptolemaic palaces now lie underwater and beneath the large concrete blocks that have been positioned to act as a breakwater. In 1995 it was announced that a team of underwater archaeologists had discovered Cleopatra's palaces. This conclusion was made following the identification of two granite sphinxes, which, it was claimed, had the portrait features of Cleopatra's father (Goddio and Claus eds. 2006: 56; Kiss 1998: 169–88). The sphinxes were found with a statue of a Roman priest holding a figure of the god Osiris-Canopus. As the initial publication of this particular piece indicates, this type of statue was produced only in the Roman period (Dunand 1998: 189–94). The identity of the sphinxes is also, in my opinion, tenuous. The facial features are more typical of the generic form of sphinx that appears in the early Roman period (Ashton 2002b), and do not resemble the distinctive portrait type of Cleopatra's father. The dating of this complex should remain more cautious; the evidence suggests that the material remains date to the early Roman period rather than exclusively to the reign of Cleopatra VII as suggested.

Caesar himself dedicated a tomb to Pompey, the Roman general who was murdered by Ptolemy XIII and whose head was presented to Caesar, soon after he landed in Alexandria in 48 BCE. The tomb had fallen into ruin by the time of the Emperor Hadrian's visit to the Egyptian capital in 130 BCE. Hadrian repaired the building and rededicated it.

5.3 TALES AND PERCEPTIONS

The decadence of the Ptolemaic royal court was infamous amongst Roman writers. Luxury (*Tryphe*) had been seen as a positive trait amongst the Hellenistic dynasts (Smith 1988: 52), but was shown as part of Antony's downfall by many Roman analysts (Plutarch, *Life of Antony* 28). The Ptolemaic court and all that it stood for offered a stark contrast to the comparatively modest lifestyle of Octavian. The fact that the Imperial house developed into an example that could well have outclassed the Ptolemaic court seems not to have mattered for the later writers.

Even Caesar had been captivated by Cleopatra's wealth, which seems to go some way to explaining how the Roman general might be captivated by the queen (Lucan, *Pharsalia* 123–200). Egypt's decadence takes up a substantial section of Lucan's work: "The beams were bound with golden coverings; no scant veneer lay on its walls, but built in solid blocks of marble, gleamed the palace" (trans. Joyce 1993: 135–8). Slaves of many nations, wine, and meat from animals sacred to Egypt completed the decadence (150–200).

Pliny the Elder refers to luxury in the Ptolemaic court with respect to the largest pearls in history and Cleopatra's banquet with Mark Antony. Cleopatra is said to have claimed that she would pay 10,000,000 sesterces for a single banquet. Pliny explains how:

> In accordance with previous instructions the servants placed in front of her a single vessel containing vinegar, the strong rough quality of which can melt pearls. She was at that moment wearing in her ears that remarkable and truly unique work of nature. Antony was full of curiosity to see what in the world she would do. She took off one earring and dropped the pearl into the vinegar and when it was melted swallowed it.

The story is clearly a fictitious one and it has been suggested that vinegar may have been used in order to retrieve the pearl more easily (*Natural Histories* 11. Loeb edition: 224 section 121). However, the story serves as an example of the decadence of the Ptolemaic court. Pliny uses the opportunity to comment that the wager was not the only battle that Antony would lose.

In book 4 chapter 29 Athenaeus states that here his source is Socrates the Rhodian who, in the third book of his *Civil War*, recounted the entertainment offered by the last queen of Egypt. The gifts to her guests included Ethiopian lamp bearers and furniture from the banquets and the plates from which they had dined (6.229c). When Cleopatra realized that the Romans were copying her decadent lifestyle, she downgraded her gold and silver dinnerware to "regular ware" thus implying that using gold and silver tableware was the norm (Thompson 2003: 83–4).

Plutarch (*Life of Antony* 28) recounted the amazement of the physician Philotas of Amphissa at seeing the amount of food being prepared for a small royal banquet in the city. This passage also makes reference to the Inimitable Livers Association, which was hosted by Cleopatra and Mark Antony. Remarkably a statue base has survived, which records the same association (see below).

To the Roman writers and historians the concept of luxury equaled Cleopatra's selfish attitude to those around her. In *Jewish Antiquities* 14–15 Josephus wrote "nothing was enough for this extravagant woman. She was enslaved by her appetite so that the whole world failed to satisfy the desires of her imagination." After describing how Cleopatra had murdered most of her family, Josephus (4.1.88) also comments:

> For the sake of any money, which there was the slightest hope of getting, both temples and tombs were violated. No sacred place was considered so inviolable that it did not have its furnishings removed and there was no secular place that did not suffer every kind of forbidden treatment so long as it was likely to satisfy to the full the greed of this wicked woman. In sum, nothing was enough for this extravagant woman, who was enslaved by her appetite, so that the whole world failed to satisfy the desires of her imagination.

5.4 SCHOLARSHIP UNDER CLEOPATRA

It is important to remember that Cleopatra's Alexandria was a city of discontent, trouble, and occupation. References to the early years of her co-rule with Ptolemy XIII demonstrate that the fires that were started by the Romans in order to regain control destroyed a substantial part of what had formed the center of the city. These fires damaged the famous library of Alexandria. The city had once been a magnet for scholars from all over the Greek world and, during the early Ptolemaic period many of the famous poets, playwrights, scientists, philosophers, and mathematicians had enjoyed Ptolemaic royal patronage as part of the Mouseion. These days had long disappeared in the years preceding the reigns of Ptolemy XII and Cleopatra VII. However, there is some evidence of a renaissance during the last years of Ptolemaic rule, which perhaps prompted Antony to replenish the contents of the damaged library by awarding Cleopatra the scrolls from Alexandria's once rival – the library of Pergamon in modern day Turkey (Plutarch, *Life of Antony* 58; Fraser 1972: vol. 1, 335 and vol. 2, 494 n.299). The Mouseion was still home to philosophers during the last years of Ptolemaic rule, scholars such as Eudoros who wrote commentaries on earlier philosophical works (Fraser 1972: vol. 1, 334–5). Others such as Potamon of Alexandria and Ainesidemos of Knossos wrote about and developed new philosophical aspects (Chauveau 2000: 174). Unlike earlier periods when the scholars were under the control of the royal house, the academics of Cleopatra's Alexandria seem to have felt no commitment to their rulers (Chauveau 2000: 175).

The Alexandrian philosopher Dion, who had played a key role in the exile of Ptolemy XII, also accompanied Cleopatra to Rome and became the teacher of Octavian. Dion only returned to Egypt following Cleopatra's defeat and was said to have urged his former pupil to have Ptolemy Caesar put to death. Others such as Philostratos, who was one of Cleopatra's advisors, changed allegiance following her death (Chauveau 2000: 175).

5.5 BEYOND THE CAPITAL CITY

The temples and images of Cleopatra are discussed in detail elsewhere in the present publication with regard to her role as ruler, regent and goddess. It is perhaps worth considering the development of Cleopatra's dedications across her roles and summarizing her affiliations with regard to her political and religious policies. Although there is no physical trace of Cleopatra at Memphis, it seems likely that she would have continued to seek the advice and support of the priesthood there in the same way that her father had forged a strong relationship with this particular group. Outside Alexandria, Cleopatra's main temple dedications were all in Upper Egypt. As noted, many were at sites that had been started by Auletes, but the Queen's loyalty lay strictly with her son and the dynasty's future. Rather than associating herself with her father, the temples of Denderah and Armant produced decorative schemes that promoted Cleopatra's son. Her cult was of course celebrated in all Egyptian temples, as indicated by the graffito at the temple of Isis at Philae, which notes that the statue of Cleopatra there had been regilded (Quaegebeur 1988: 41).

Cleopatra by no means restricted her patronage to new projects in Alexandria. A stela dedicated to the Buchis bull indicates that the queen took a personal interest in Egyptian cults. As already noted, the queen was said to have rowed the new bull to its home, suggesting that she was present, perhaps even on the boat carrying the new god. However, to what extent this language was merely formulaic is not known. The decoration of the temple of Hathor at Denderah has already been discussed in some detail, and the smaller projects at Armant and Koptos were also substantial with respect to their religious significance. It is notable that, unlike for her father and his predecessors, there are no remains of Cleopatra at Karnak, the largest and most powerful of the temple complexes in Egypt.

As already discussed, Cleopatra was said to have taken Caesar up the Nile to see Upper Egypt and its temples. This journey can be interpreted in two ways: firstly, that Cleopatra wished to show the Roman general the wealth of her country and also her heritage; or secondly that the Romans wished to assert their power and claim to Egypt. Perhaps the truth lay somewhere between the two. Suetonius (*Deified Julius Caesar* 52.1) claimed that Caesar did not allow his army to accompany him and that the pair sailed almost as far as Ethiopia (probably meaning Sudan/Nubia).

Ptolemais or Egyptian Psoi maintained an important position until the end of the Ptolemaic period. Strabo said it was the largest village in the Thebaid and comparable to Memphis in size (17.1.42, 46), where it has been estimated (Thompson 1988: 50) around 50,000 people were resident. Today, there are few visible remains at the site, which is situated close to the modern city of Sohag. The city acted as an administrative center for the south of Egypt and is well attested in documentation from the Ptolemaic period. The site lost its importance during the Roman occupation, but remained occupied. It would be interesting to know whether the city was Greek or Egyptian in appearance, particularly following the recent discoveries of Egyptian-style sculpture and architecture in its northern counterpart Alexandria. Together these two Greek cities represent Cleopatra's role as mistress of the two lands. Whether the southern city was patronized by the queen, in addition to the traditional Egyptian temples, remains to be seen and can only really be determined through further investigation of the site and its remains.

6

CLEOPATRA AS A GODDESS

6.1 THE DEVELOPMENT OF RELIGIOUS POLICY THROUGH THE PTOLEMAIC QUEENS

In the context of the present book it seems more relevant to review religious developments through the royal female line (for further details see Ashton 2003a: 115–42). Following their death Ptolemy I and Berenice I were deified by their son Ptolemy II. Their cult, as the Theoi Soteres (Savior Gods), was established in Alexandria but was independent of the cult of Alexander. Indeed the cult of the Theoi Soteres was not joined to the main dynastic cult of Alexander until the reforms of Ptolemy IV (Hölbl 2001:169–70; Fraser 1972: vol. 1, 218), when a new tomb for Alexander was built, which included a pyramid over the top (Lucan viii. 692–9; Fraser 1972: vol. 1, 16; vol. 2, 35 n.83). This dynastic cult was Greek in character. The priest of Alexander and subsequent Ptolemies, together with the priestesses of the various queens, were used in all official and legal dating formulae. The Egyptian dynastic cult that is found in Egyptian temples and other contexts were a very different entity. A relief at the temple of Horus at Edfu illustrates the lineage of the Ptolemaic dynastic cult well (Plate 6.1).

Arsinoe II is the first notable female of the dynasty. She was the sister and second wife of Ptolemy II and ruled with her brother from around 275–270 BCE. There was a second ruler cult for Ptolemy II and Arsinoe II as the Theoi Adelphoi (Sibling Gods) that was, unlike that of their parents, attached to the Alexandrian dynastic cult of Alexander. Following his sister's

Plate 6.1 Relief showing the dynastic cults, temple of Horus at Edfu

death Ptolemy II established a cult of Arsinoe II with a special basket-bearing priestess called the Kanephoros who joined the dynastic cult of Alexander. New temples were dedicated to Arsinoe in Alexandria, the Fayoum, and elsewhere in Egypt. Sanctuaries were also built in Ptolemaic possessions overseas. A tholos (round temple) was dedicated by Ptolemy II to his sister at Samothrace in Greece for example. Arsinoe appears in the relief decoration of the temple of the Egyptian goddess Isis at Philae (Plate 6.2) as a fully developed member of the Egyptian pantheon. She stands behind Isis receiving an offering from her brother/consort Ptolemy II, wearing her distinctive crown and her name written in hieroglyphs in a cartouche. Text references show that the queen's temples in the Fayoum were distinct from those of the Theoi Adelphoi (Quaegebeur, 1988: 43–4; Fraser 1972: vol. 1, 228). In addition to their own temples, these new gods also became temple-sharing gods. A temple-sharing god, in Greek *sunnaos theos*, lived in temples dedicated to other principal deities. This was a cost-effective means of establishing a new cult

Plate 6.2 Relief showing Arsinoe II, temple of Isis Philae

rather than building new temples. A cult would be allocated a priest or be tended by the existing priests rather than new temples being constructed in honor of the new god. Towns were also named after these new gods.

In the dating formulae Ptolemy III always refers to the Theoi Adelphoi as his parents, even though his mother was Arsinoe I; his immediate acceptance of the queen and willingness to be associated with her can be seen on the gateway in front of the temple of Khonsu at Karnak (Plate 6.3), where Ptolemy III offers to his father Ptolemy II and aunt/step-mother Arsinoe II. In the second century BCE, following the death of Ptolemy VI, Cleopatra II continued to rule with Ptolemy VIII but the king took a second wife, his niece and the daughter of Cleopatra II – Cleopatra III. In 132/1 BCE Cleopatra II organized a revolt against her brother and declared herself queen in Upper Egypt, taking the titles Queen Cleopatra, Philometor (mother-loving) goddess, Soteira (the savior), thus resurrecting the title that she used with Ptolemy VI (Whitehorne 1994: 118).

Plate 6.3 Relief from the Khonsu gateway, Karnak

Cleopatra III took her divine status a step further than previous queens had been permitted (Ashton 2003a: 126, 138–42). Dating formulae on papyri indicate that she believed herself to be Isis. She also adopted the priestly roles, such as priest of the cult of Alexander, a role typically held by the male ruler. The queen claimed five out of the nine Alexandrian eponymous priesthoods for her own cults (Hölbl 2001: 280, 285). Her image also reveals an ambitious response to her individual power: Cleopatra III can be found to take the dominant position on relief scenes, standing in front of Ptolemy IX, her son, in an offering scene at Karnak temple (Quaegebeur 1988: 51, n.60) and in the mammisi at Deir el Medina (Plate 4.8). Her power was also expressed through sculpture, where she adopted a more masculine image. This observation holds in both her Greek- and Egyptian-style representations (Walker and Higgs eds. 2001: 59–60). It is not clear, however, whether this was simply copying the portrait type of her male co-rulers or whether it was representative of her personal power and a means of presenting her in a more appropriate masculine fashion

(Ashton 2001a: 44; 2003a: 140–1). Ptolemaic queens do not generally seem to have felt it necessary to be shown in the guise of a male pharaoh in order to promote their power. Elevation was indicated by the adoption of male titles in the feminine, for example "female Horus," a title adopted by Berenice II, a queen who was not obviously powerful either politically or in cultic terms until after her death (Ashton 2003a: 79–81, 112–13).

6.2 CLEOPATRA VII IN EGYPT

Ptolemaic royals could be deified in a number of ways. Initially the rulers were associated with an established deity; it was a modest way in which to elevate royal status. Such caution was necessary in the Greek world, where living gods were not generally acceptable. One exception to this observation was of course Alexander, although it is not known for certain that the ruler presented himself as a god to the Greeks during his life (Smith 1988: 39, 40, 110). From the time of Ptolemy II, a closer link was made between living ruler and deceased parents through the award of a posthumous cult of the latter. Ptolemies were accepted as divine and venerated in a dynastic cult that incorporated the ruling couple together with their forebears. Similarly, in the case of the women, a ruler could also be awarded a personal cult; in the third century BCE this was posthumous. By the reign of Cleopatra I, however, rulers were well-established as gods during their lifetimes and this Cleopatra was not only the first with this name but was also the first royal female to act successfully as regent and to be shown as a goddess in her own right during her lifetime (Ashton 2003a: 129).

As an Egyptian ruler Cleopatra VII served a divine role and was an intermediary between the traditional Egyptian gods and the people. This occupation came with a number of important responsibilities and required careful leadership of the Egyptian priesthood. Cleopatra seems to have taken her position seriously and have thrown herself enthusiastically into her role as both ruler and goddess.

The queen was presented as a divine being from the start of her reign. A stela dating to year 1 of her solo rule (Bianchi 1988: 188–9, no. 78; Walker and Higgs eds. 2001: 156–7) includes the title "Thea," which is Greek for goddess. The stela is dedicated on behalf of Cleopatra and reads: "On behalf of Queen Cleopatra, goddess, father-loving, the (holy) place of the association of (Isis) Snonaitiake, of whom the president is the chief priest (*lesonis*) Onnophris. Year 1, Epeiph 1 (July 2, 51 BC)" (Rowlandson ed. 1998: 37–8). As noted, attention has focused on the image at the top of this carved relief; a male pharaoh offers to Isis and Horus. Earlier royal women, such as the God's Wives of Amun (see chapter 3) were shown wearing the divine vulture headdress. This does not usually seem to have been the case for Cleopatra VII. Her titles indicate that there was no question with regard to her divinity; however, the majority of representations show the queen as a ruler and not a goddess. The exceptions to this observation will be discussed in greater detail below.

6.3 CLEOPATRA'S DIVINE TITLES

It was through her Greek titles that Cleopatra's divinity was expressed. Greek titles were more flexible than their Egyptian counterparts and, although the Egyptian priests were able to write Greek epithets such as "father-loving" in hieroglyphs, just as they later wrote "Caesar," they do not seem to have used the title "New Isis," preferring to use already established titles (chapter 4). Nor was it necessary to call Cleopatra a goddess; her status as ruler of Egypt indicated that she was divine according to Egyptian theology as a female Horus. The gods with whom the queen was associated in her names often copy those of the earlier Arsinoe II. These associations, along with her temple-building programme, allow us some insight into Cleopatra's divine affiliations.

The Egyptian titles of Cleopatra have already been noted with respect to her position as ruler. The majority were concerned with her role as ruler and prominent royal female. One title, however, describes the queen as the Daughter of Geb (Troy 1986: A1/7), a title used by Arsinoe II, who wore a crown modeled on that of the god Geb. Cleopatra VII adopted this same crown on a stela in the Turin Museum (Ashton 2001a: 48), and on a single relief on the inner walls of the temple of Hathor at Denderah (Plate 4.13).

As noted, with regard to her Greek titles in Egypt, Cleopatra was called Thea Neotera (the newer goddess). The queen takes the longer titles Thea Neotera Philopator kai Philopatris in year 17 of her reign (the newer goddess, who loves her father and her country) (Bingen 2007: 76). The adoption of the newer goddess is thought to have been linked to Cleopatra Thea.

6.4 CLEOPATRA'S DIVINE STATUES

Cleopatra's personal cult lasted until 373 CE, nearly 350 years after her death, as attested by a demotic inscription reading "I overlaid the figure of Cleopatra with gold" (Quaegebeur 1988: 41). This cult statue would have been a small wooden figure and would have been treated not as a representation but as a god. As with many of her ancestors Cleopatra VII would have been a temple-sharing god. There are two small wooden statues of a divine figure bearing a cartouche with the name Cleopatra written in hieroglyphics (Ashton 2001a: 65, 2.3 and 102–3 cat. 41; Bianchi 2003: 16–17, pls. 2–3). The first, now in Seattle Art Museum, is a complete painted figure measuring 30 centimeters in height in the form of a seated female wearing a dress that is tied beneath the breasts, exposing the nipples in an unprecedented manner. The goddess wears a wig, the crown of Hathor/Isis in the form of a sun-disk, and cow's horns, and has the remains of a cobra on her brow.

The second statue, formerly in the Stafford collection, is larger in scale measuring 23 centimeters and preserved only in the form of a bust. The decoration is carved and there are no traces of pigment on the surface. The subject wears a collar, an echeloned wig with the base of a crown in the form of a circlet of cobras. On the brow is a double uraeus with the crowns of Upper and Lower Egypt on each of the cobras and in the center is a vulture head in copper alloy. The eyes are inlaid with calcite and what is recorded as lapis lazuli, but which may be blue glass. The authenticity of both the inscriptions and also the statues has rightly been questioned, but perhaps these two wooden figures offer an idea of the form that the Philae cult statue mentioned in the demotic graffito of Cleopatra VII might have taken.

There is a group of stone statues that may represent Cleopatra VII as a goddess. This group is distinct from those discussed in chapter 4 in that they have Greek-style features, adopting one or more of the following: a corkscrew wig, a cornucopia (horn of plenty), and the styling of the drapery. The figures also wear a specific style of dress, which has two components and is knotted either above or between the breasts. This form of dress is Egyptian in style (Bianchi 1980), but on occasion it appears with a style of drapery that is more commonly found on Greek-style representations. This type of statue was used in the Roman period to represent the goddess Isis (Ashton 2004a: 49–50). The reason for believing these statues to be divine rather than royal images is that there is an earlier inscribed representation of this form, which includes the epithet "goddess" after the name of the queen – the aforementioned statue of Arsinoe II now housed in the Metropolitan Museum, New York (Plate 4.3; Walker and Higgs 2001: 166–7, no. 166; Ashton 2001a: 45–53, for discussion of this group).

The first example to be associated with Cleopatra can be linked to the above wooden figures in that it has a cartouche spelling Cleopatra in hieroglyphs. The statue (Plate 6.4) is without a provenance and is now housed in the Metropolitan Museum of Art in New York (Walker and Higgs 2001: 165, no. 164; Ashton 2001a: 41–2, 116–17, no. 65, cat. 64; Stanwick 2002: 80, 125, E14). The statue is of a slightly smaller scale than the other Egyptian-style representations associated with the queen,

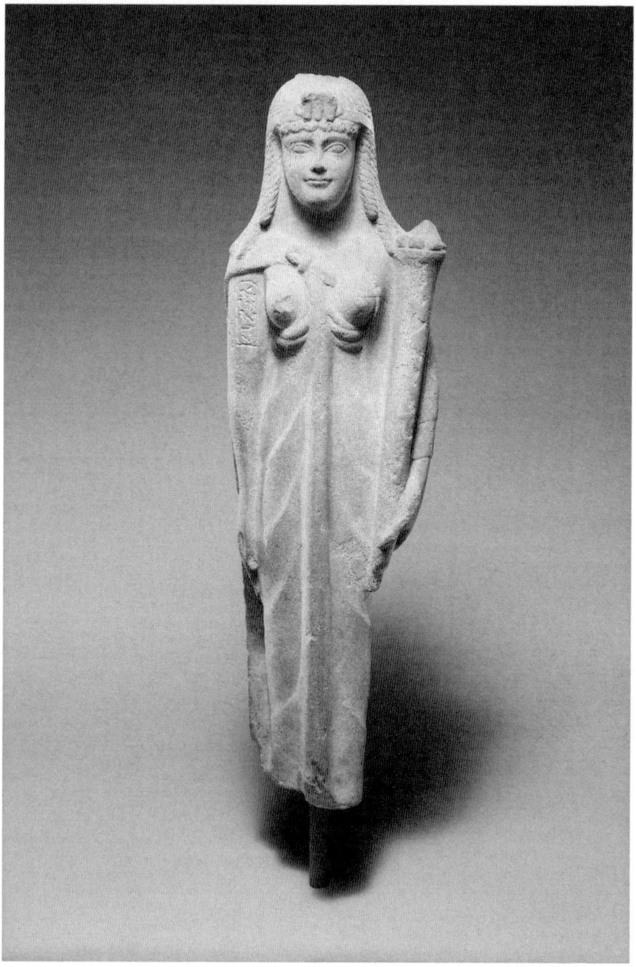

Plate 6.4 Marble statue of Cleopatra VII. Metropolitan Museum, New York, inv. 89.2.660

which show Cleopatra as a ruler/queen. It is made from Proconnesian marble, a type commonly used in Roman Alexandria (Ashton 2001a: 49 n.266). Like the other statues, this example has a high back pillar that would have originally supported a crown. The left hand holds a single cornucopia and the right

Plate 6.5 Limestone statue of Cleopatra VII. Brooklyn Museum. 71.12. Charles Edwin Wilbour Fund

hand is, unusually, placed flat against the side of the thigh rather than holding the so-called enigmatic bar in the usual Egyptian fashion. As with the two wooden statues the authenticity of the cartouche has been questioned (Bianchi 2003: 17–18) on account of the orientation of the signs and the form of the fourth sign, which should be shown as a lasso but is actually a snake. The cartouche, therefore, may have been a later, modern addition. This statue is similar than a more fragmentary piece now in the Brooklyn Museum of Art (Plate 6.5; Walker and Higgs 2001: 164, no. 163; Ashton 2001a: 49–50, 116–17, no. 64; Stanwick 2002: 80, 124–25, E13). Both statues have identical hairstyles: a series of corkscrew locks with a row of snail-shell curls forming a fringe and a triple uraeus on a plain diadem. The curls and diadem accord with the Roman-style marble heads of Cleopatra

(Higgs 2001: 203–7) and the queen's coinage. The eyes of the Brooklyn statue were originally inlaid and the overall appearance is one of a youthful female, with rounded cheeks, fleshy down-turned lips, and a small nose. Its execution and style is wholly Egyptian. The back pillar would also once have supported a crown. The carving of the Metropolitan statue is quite different in terms of its more angular, less carefully carved features. The eyes of the Metropolitan queen differ in that they are carved rather than inlaid, but are still proportionately large. The mouth of the Metropolitan representation is down-turned in the manner of many of the statues in this group, but the lips have a much "tighter" appearance. The use of three cobras is comparable to the practice found in the group of statues already discussed as representations of Cleopatra VII in chapter 4.

Within the proposed group of divine images, it is worth considering a further statue of similar form, with corkscrew locks and a knotted garment, wearing a diadem. This statue was dated to the first century BCE on stylistic grounds and because of the high form of the back pillar, which is paralleled on many of the statues with a triple uraeus (Ashton 2001a: 114–15, cat. 62). This piece is now in the gardens of the Greco-Roman Museum in Alexandria and is one of the few to have a known provenance; it was found at Canopus, east of Alexandria and an area connected to the capital city by the reign of Cleopatra VII. It is colossal in size, measuring 2.35 meters from the knees to the head, and carved out of granite. The arms and chest area are badly damaged and the face appears to have been deliberately hacked away from the head. There is a face from a similar statue housed in a private collection. One curl too many is preserved on the head meaning that it could not possibly fit the Alexandrian statue, but the scale and style of the piece suggest that it came from a similar representation, perhaps even the same workshop. The head is youthful in appearance and has a more naturalistic style of "portrait" than the other Egyptian-style representations. It is comparable with the Roman statues of Cleopatra VII already mentioned, in particular the heads now in the Vatican and Berlin (Plates 3.12 and 3.13).

Plate 6.6 Basalt statue of Cleopatra VII. Egyptian Museum, Turin, inv. C.1385. © Museo Antichità Egizie di Torino

A more traditional Egyptian-style statue, now in the Egyptian Museum, Turin, has also been linked to Cleopatra VII (Walker and Higgs 2001: 168, no. 167; Ashton 2001a: 39, 100–1, no. 38; Stanwick 2002: 80, 127, F5 – possibly Cleopatra VII). This statue is not in the same form as the previous examples mentioned in this chapter, but shows the queen with a youthful portrait, similar to that of the Brooklyn Museum's statue. The mouth is down-turned, the chin is prominent, and the face is broad with rounded cheeks (Plate 6.6). She wears a sheath-like dress, as indicated by the fine seam collar at the neck. Her wig is an echeloned tripartite form and on top are the stylized wings of a vulture (a divine headdress). On her brow are three figures; one would expect the central one to be a vulture head but it appears to be the same as the flanking royal cobras. Perhaps this is a queen wearing a triple uraeus. In that case a fourth element of a vulture may have been too absurd to add; reference to this was found in the wig. At the top of the head is a fragment of a base for a crown. This particular statue is very similar to the representation of Ptolemy XV from the temple dedicated to Julius Caesar in Alexandria; there may have been a deliberate link between the two. The statue has been dated to the third century BCE on grounds of the portrait (Walker and Higgs 2001: 168–9). Such a conclusion does not take into account the retrospective images that re-emerged during the reign of Cleopatra VII. The statue is also unique in that no other examples of representations of Ptolemaic queens use the traditional vulture in order to indicate that the image is that of a god. Only on the temple reliefs of the deceased Arsinoe II does the vulture cap appear (Plate 6.2).

6.5 ISIS

As noted, Cleopatra VII's Great Grandmother, Cleopatra III, believed herself to be a living embodiment of the goddess Isis (Ashton 2003a: 118–19). This was the next stage in the development of the deification of the Ptolemaic royal women. As noted, so godlike was Cleopatra III that she had a number of cults dedicated solely to her worship. This was a woman of power who was positioned in front of her son on the walls of the Deir el Medina mammisi (Plate 4.8), and a woman who not only adopted a masculine portrait type, but also took on roles that had previously been restricted to men, such as the Priest of the Cult of Alexander and the Ptolemies. Royal women had long been linked to the Hathoric elements of queenship and, as mother of the king, had naturally been associated with the goddess Isis, mother of Horus, for whom the living ruler was the living embodiment on earth. For Cleopatra III to state that she was Isis is slightly different to the more established association and, in the case of Cleopatra VII, the idea of a "New Isis" implies special powers and a rebirth of a standard goddess. The concept of a "new" (in Greek *Neos* or *Nea*) god was one that continued into the Roman Imperial period. Ptolemy XII, Cleopatra's father, believed himself to be the New Dionysos and Cleopatra's Isis is likely to have been influenced by her father's cult.

The problem with identifying statues of Cleopatra as the New Isis is finding a feature to distinguish her from the many regular representations of the goddess. In Plutarch's description of the Donations of Alexandria (an event of international importance discussed further on pp. 158–61), Cleopatra is said to have worn the sacred garment of Isis and to have born the title New Isis (*Life of Antony* 54.5–9; Jones 2006: 116). The form of the garment of Isis is not known. It is possible that this refers to a crown or headdress rather than a dress. During this period Isis typically wore a sheath-like garment, which was found on representations of women in general. A knotted shawl often referred to as an "Isis knot" was not introduced to this particular goddess's iconography until the end of the first century CE (Bianchi 1980; Ashton 2000; 2004c: 56). Her guise, in the form of Isis, on this occasion indicates that the donations were ceremonial rather than simply political.

We are extremely fortunate to have the surviving image of Cleopatra as Isis from the Alexandrian temple of Isis (Plate 4.18). It is a traditional Egyptian-style representation revealing a youthful face and is colossal in size. It was part of a dyad, the male figure representing Ptolemy XV. The surviving section from the bust to the base of the crown is 3 meters high. The queen wears an echeloned wig, a circlet of cobras base for a crown, and a vulture cap. There seems to have been a single vulture head at the front of the headdress. The statue is quite remarkable and it is fair to say that photographs do not do it justice. Now housed in the Royal Museum of Mariemont and displayed on a wall within the Egyptian galleries, at a considerable height but still lower than it would have originally stood (on account of the architecture!), it is possible to view the piece from below and from a first-floor level balcony. What is so notable about this particular statue, in addition to its scale, is that the eyes are carved so that they look directly at the viewer in a manner that is unusual for Egyptian sculptures. The hands are also preserved in

Belgium and are unusual in that they are clasped, showing equal status of the two subjects. Sadly, the lower section, which was sketched in the late 1900s is now missing. Without the accompanying male statue, which shows Ptolemy XV (some think Ptolemy XII) as a ruler, it would be impossible to distinguish this statue from images of Isis. Here Cleopatra protects her son. The two, as equals, hold hands (Ashton 2007b).

In 1841 Wilkinson identified the above statues of Cleopatra and Ptolemy XV as representations of a king as Osiris (Plate 4.17), and so the deceased king, with an image of his queen as Isis (172; Plate 4.18). The female statue is an idealized representation of Isis, who is identified by her crown and by the vulture cap on her head. Her costume is the usual generic sheath-like dress worn by royal women and goddesses alike. As noted the male statue has a youthful face and wears the traditional *nemes* headcloth. The association was made on account of what was interpreted as a crook (*crux ansata*), but which could equally be a flail held in the left hand of the statue, across the left shoulder; we are totally dependent upon a sketch provided by Harris, the British Consul, and included in a letter by Joseph Bonomi to Sir John Gardner Wilkinson written on October 18, 1842, for this information. The torso of the male ruler is now missing, although the tip of the scepter or flail is just about visible on the shoulder of the statue, now preserved in the Greco-Roman museum. One of the main problems with accepting this statue as a representation of the king as Osiris is the *nemes* headcloth; kings usually wear the *atef* crown when they are depicted as the god (Ashton 2004b: 548–9). The drawings also show that the male ruler once wore what is known as a *hm.hmt* crown. This particular headdress was often worn by the living king and was also associated with the young Horus (later known as Harpocrates). It therefore seems plausible that the pair represents Cleopatra as Isis, perhaps even in her guise of the new Isis, and her son as the young Horus. Others have suggested that the statue might represent her father Ptolemy XII as Osiris (Stanwick 2002: 18). The statues would have originally stood at around 9 meters in height and make a strong cultural statement: that the reigning rulers were Egyptian.

The site associated with the Isis temple has been lost to modern development and has received little attention from scholars working on Cleopatra VII, probably because most have been historians rather than archaeologists. In 2003 (Ashton 2001b: 120–2; 2003: 120–2) it was suggested that the mausoleum was located close to the find spot of the statues on account of the identification of the Isis sanctuary. A full discussion of the nature of the site will be published as part of a volume of conference proceedings (Ashton 2007b). I will provide a summary below.

The site now identified as the Isis temple appears on nineteenth-century maps outside and to the east of the main walls of Alexandria and is called a variety of different names including temple, ruins, statues, and Telesterion (a sanctuary of the Greek goddess Demeter). One government map has a sketch of the area, on the banks of Lake Hadra, and includes columns, sphinxes, and statue fragments. Contemporary descriptions of the site record similar features and many travelers refer to the large size of the associated structures that were cut into the bedrock; they also mention the colossal statues, sphinxes, and, in one instance, that there was a round temple (Ashton 2007b). This particular feature is significant because this form of building was directly associated with the Ptolemaic royal cults, in particular those dedicated to Arsinoe II at Samothrace and in Alexandria. A sketch by Lepsius (1842: vol. 1, 2) recorded an additional statue in the form of a granite elephant, now housed in the Kunsthistorishes Museum, Vienna. The sanctuary seems to have contained a mixture of Greek and Egyptian elements and to have been of considerable size and importance. The site was excavated in 1892 when Botti, the Director of the Greco-Roman Museum in Alexandria, recorded Nineteenth- and Twenty-sixth Dynasty sphinxes, probably those that had been described by the early travelers. This indicates that earlier material was moved to the site, most probably to enhance its Egyptian nature, perhaps originally from the abandoned temple at Heliopolis.1 This practice was not uncommon in the Ptolemaic period and became fashionable later under the Romans, who shipped Egyptian artifacts to Rome (Ashton 2004a: 48–9 and 2007a).

In November 2004 a British–Belgian team, working with the help of the Centre d'Etudes Alexandrines, undertook a geophysical survey of an area that had been identified as a possible location for the sanctuary, by comparing the nineteenth century maps of Smyth and Falaki (Ashton 2005b: 30–2). The results were mixed, largely on account of interference from parked vehicles, the surrounding road, the compacted surface, and saline water levels from where the lake had been filled. In spite of these problems, in one particular area several anomalies were identified and included what may be a 30 meter by 30 meter corner of a wall. The identification of the underground features is dependent upon opening a trench to confirm that the structures are ancient. An application at the time of writing has been placed with the Egyptian Supreme Council of Antiquities but is dependent upon gaining access to areas that are now privately owned. An exhibition is planned at the Royal Museum of Mariemont in 2010. There is still much of Cleopatra's to discover, reassess, and understand. Considering the queen within her correct context is a good place from which to start.

6.6 UNIVERSAL GODDESS

Cleopatra also appeared as a goddess in Rome. The first reference, as already noted, is to a statue in the temple of Venus Genetrix, which was said to have been dedicated by Julius Caesar but which, sadly, does not survive. Appian (*Civil War* 2.102) wrote the following with regard to the statue: "He [Julius Caesar] set up a beautiful statue of Cleopatra next to the statue of the goddess [Venus]; it still stands there today [early second century CE]." Some modern scholars have speculated that the head of Cleopatra now held in the Vatican museums, which has a small additional section of stone on the cheek, was modeled on the original and that the attachment is where the finger of Ptolemy XV touched his mother's cheek, in the style of Aphrodite and Eros (Higgs 2001: 204 for discussion).

Another statue of Venus has also been associated with Cleopatra. The statue is a Roman copy of a Hellenistic original that is now housed in the Monte Martini annex of the Capitoline museums. It has been argued that the statue was commissioned during the reign of the Emperor Claudius, who was the grandson of Mark Antony (Moreno 1994; Higgs 2001: 208–9 for discussion). More recently (2006) an exhibition has been designed around the piece and it has been suggested that the statue is a direct copy of the image of Cleopatra that stood in the temple of Venus Genetrix in Rome (Andreae 2006: 14–47). The statue, known as the Esquiline Venus, takes the form of a naked female wearing a Greek *stephane* (crown), her hair tied back into a bun. By her side is a water jar with a snake coiled around the exterior (hence the suggested link to Cleopatra through her possible means of suicide); the subject's dress is thrown over the vessel. In the earlier 2001 Cleopatra exhibition catalogue (Walker and Higgs 2001: 208–9) the identification was disputed on account of the harsh modeling of the facial features. Nevertheless, many characteristics are shared with the recognized Roman-style images of Cleopatra that are housed in the Vatican and Berlin Museums. The snake is certainly a later addition, perhaps to the copy following the death of the queen, and would accord with the Roman written sources, who discuss the statue of Cleopatra that was carried as part of Octavian's victory parade. The statue may therefore be a hybrid of the temple statue and be that carried in the victory parade.

One of the most remarkable representations of Cleopatra was found near a sanctuary of Isis in Rome and is now likewise housed at the Monte Martini annex of the Capitoline Museums (Plate 5.1 Walker and Higgs 2001: 216–17, no. 194). The head was re-used as masonry fill for the building of the Church of San Pietro and Marcellino on the Via Labicana. The associated Roman sanctuary of Isis was dedicated by the Triumvirs Mark Antony, Octavian, and Lepidus, who formed their alliance in 43 BCE. The head is made from imported Parian marble and would have been slotted into the body of a statue in a style typical of the Hellenistic Alexandrian school. The "portrait" features are very similar to those of the other Classical representations of Cleopatra from Rome (see chapter 4). The overall appearance is youthful and idealized. However, certain features are shared with even the Egyptian-style representations, most notably the definition of the chin and fleshy lips. The nose has been damaged but a profile view of the statue indicates that it was substantial in size, probably not dissimilar to the images of Cleopatra's father. The statue was made according to classical artistic conventions, but has Egyptian-style iconographic features in the form of a traditional echeloned wig and an intricately carved vulture headdress. The head of the vulture is now missing but would have been added, most probably, in copper alloy (bronze), gold, or silver; however, there are no traces of corrosion products or adhesive in the hole. There would also have been a small Egyptian-style crown slotted into the top of the head. The form would probably have been the usual crown of Isis, which consisted of cow's horns and sun-disk. The hole here is relatively shallow, which suggests that the proportions were smaller than those usually adhered to by Egyptian artists. It is precisely these manufacturing anomalies that make this statue fragment so intriguing and make it difficult to determine with any certainty which school was responsible for its manufacture – Egyptian, Hellenistic Greek, or Roman. It is the first example of a representation made according to Classical canons that incorporates or mimics Egyptian features and is therefore Egyptianizing (Walker and Higgs 2001: 216–17 no. 194; Ashton 2003a: 122). It has been suggested that the statue was carved in Egypt and brought to Rome on account of the skilful carving of the wig and vulture, alongside the typical Ptolemaic family trait of large ears, which in this instance, are positioned unevenly.

A good impression of the completed profile can be obtained from the small gold finger ring (Plate 6.7; Walker and Higgs 2001: 217, no. 195). Even on this small scale (the ring is 1.7 cm high) it is possible to determine the rounded fleshy cheeks, strong nose, and large eyes of the subject, suggesting that the image probably represents Cleopatra VII. The queen is shown in profile, wearing the traditional vulture headdress of a goddess, tri-partite

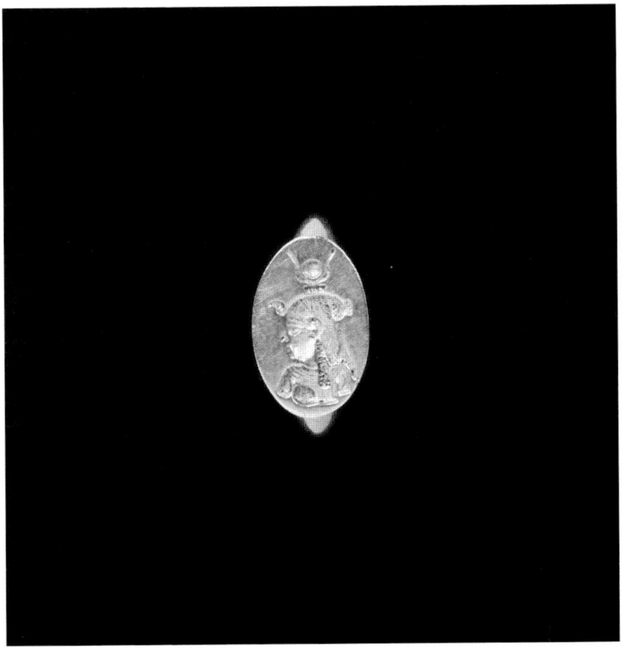

Plate 6.7 Gold ring engraved with a representation of Cleopatra VII. The Victoria and Albert Museum, London, inv. M38.1963. © Victoria and Albert Museum, London

wig, sun-disk, and cow's horns. The right breast is shown frontally – probably a reference to Isis.

Cleopatra also appeared in the guise of the goddess Aphrodite, the Greek equivalent to Isis, on coinage minted in Cyprus, a Ptolemaic possession, to celebrate the birth of her son with Julius Caesar (Plate 4.7; also Walker and Higgs 2001: 178, no. 186). Caesar restored Cyprus as a Ptolemaic possession to Cleopatra. It was perhaps for this reason that we find a unique form of numismatic representation of the queen on the island. The double cornucopia also served to link Cleopatra with Arsinoe II, her predecessor. The obverse shows a profile view of Cleopatra wearing the Greek *stephane* (a crown worn by goddesses). In front of the queen is a small blob, thought to represent her son

Ptolemy Caesar, and behind her is a scepter. In spite of the divine symbolism the legend on the reverse reads: "Cleopatra Queen." This would suggest that the role of a ruler was divine. It is noteworthy that on other coins Cleopatra wears the royal diadem, and not the divine crown, when she is shown as ruler of Egypt. The dating of this particular coin is uncertain and scholars tend to date it widely between the years 51–30 BCE, covering the entire span of her rule. It has recently been suggested that the child was not that of Julius Caesar but rather one of her later children (Kreuzer 2000: 6, 29–30). This reattribution is on account of a proposed re-dating of the coin to sometime after 39 BCE. Others have queried the chronology of Cleopatra's stay in Rome (Carcopino 1937: 48)

There were a number of coins minted in Cyprus during the reign of Cleopatra VII, on which, it has recently been suggested, the queen also wears a stephane (crown), indicating that she appears as a goddess on the obverse and the double cornucopia on the reverse (Kreuzer 2000: 41–5). These coins were hitherto dated to the reign of Ptolemy IV and were believed to show representations of Arsinoe III. However, the double cornucopia would make Arsinoe II or Cleopatra VII as more likely candidates for the representations on the obverse (Kreuzer 2000: 41). The portrait type on the illustrated examples is closer to that of Cleopatra VII. It has been suggested that this particular series of coins was begun in 38 BCE (Kreuzer 2000: 41). These suggestions have not been widely published and so have not produced an academic response from numismatists; nevertheless they are worth mentioning and deserve further consideration by scholars.

NOTE

1 I would like to thank Dorothy Thompson for suggesting this.

7

CLEOPATRA, MARK ANTONY, AND THE EAST

7.1 THE MEETING OF ANTONY AND CLEOPATRA

It is possible that Antony met the young Cleopatra when he served under the Roman general Gabinius in 55 BCE (Plutarch, *Life of Antony*: 3; Jones 2006: 95–6). Their formal meeting, following the death of Julius Caesar, is well known, although we are entirely dependent on literary sources that were written some time after the event for our evidence. One ancient author reported: "Antony was amazed at her within, as well as her good looks, and became her captive as though he were a young man, although he was forty years of age. It is said that he was always very susceptible in this way, and that he had fallen in love with her at first sight long ago when she was still a girl and he was serving as master of horse under Gabinius at Alexandria" (Appian, *Civil Wars*, book 5, ch. 8; trans. by Thackery, Loeb edition).

In chapter 25 of his *Life of Antony* Plutarch records that her reasons for meeting with Mark Antony were to answer the accusation of raising money for Gabinius and having helped him against the Triumvirs. For their official meeting at Tarsus Cleopatra presented herself as a goddess in a "ship covered in gold with purple sails and rowers pulling with silver oars and flutes accompanied by lyres." Plutarch goes on to report (26) that Cleopatra reclined under a golden canopy in the guise of the Greek goddess Aphrodite and was accompanied by boys dressed as Cupids and her maids dressed as Nereids, the winds, and Graces (Jones 2006: 99–103). Plutarch then describes (27) Antony's banquet in return.

In this way Plutarch is able to illustrate the balance of the relationship. Cleopatra is intelligent, beautiful, and in control; Antony is a soldier who can order up a dinner. The blame for his downfall as seen in the eyes of the Romans is moved from Antony, with his simple character, to Cleopatra, who is calculating.

Josephus (*Jewish Antiquities*, book 13.1.324) states simply that Cleopatra made Mark Antony a "captive of love." This contrasts with the lengthy description in Plutarch's *Life of Antony*. The idea that Antony succumbed to Cleopatra's charms at first sight is a common thread through the ancient literature (Appian, *Civil Wars*, book 5, ch. 1). Appian commented that this passion "brought ruin upon them and upon all Egypt besides," a view that may have been influenced by his own identity as an Egyptian, albeit it an Alexandrian from Roman Egypt. Appian (book 5, ch. 9) also notes that no sooner had Cleopatra won Antony's affections, then she used her position to punish her enemies, including her sister Arsinoe IV, who had been exiled at Ephesus.

7.2 RELATIONSHIP WITH ANTONY

There are two main themes that concern ancient writers on the subject of Antony and Cleopatra. The first is their relationship; here Cleopatra is seen to be responsible for the Roman's downfall. The second key theme is Cleopatra's manipulation of Antony's political power in order to obtain foreign territories. By far the most detailed discussion of Cleopatra's relationship with Mark Antony appears in Plutarch's *Life of Antony*. Antony's great passion for Cleopatra (a constant feature in the literary sources to illustrate his weakness) is referred to in chapters 32, 36, and 37. Chapter 33 notes the ominous warning by an Egyptian soothsayer to Antony, of the threat of Octavian; the repeated mention of Cleopatra, and Antony's passion for the queen, around chapter 33 can only be intended to stress to the reader the real threat that Cleopatra posed to the general. Plutarch even goes so far as to suggest that when Cleopatra was not around Antony was able to function as a strong and efficient leader. In chapter 51, when Cleopatra delayed re-joining Antony in Syria, we are told that the Roman drank heavily. Once Cleopatra had arrived Antony gave his soldiers money, claiming that it was a gift from the queen; Cleopatra, we are told, distributed clothing of her own account to the men.

The idea that Cleopatra and Egypt affected Antony's clarity of judgment and sanity is illustrated in the Roman sources by reports of his adoption of non-Roman traditions. Antony's association with Dionysos as a new form of the god and the statues commissioned by him, and of him, are all used to illustrate his demise (Plutarch, *Life of Antony* 60). The fact that Ptolemy Caesar was enrolled in the list of Alexandrian Ephebes and that both he and Antyllus were conferred a *toga virilis* supports this idea (71). It is of course impossible to know if these stories were invented to illustrate her character as perceived by the Romans, but this choice of episodes is striking.

Antony is also directly compared with his rival Octavian in the Roman sources. Plutarch, for example (*Life of Antony* 73), presents a simple psychological profile of Octavian, who is said to have been intelligent and calculating, and Cleopatra who was "conscious and intensely proud of her personal beauty." Antony, on the other hand, is shown to be jealous and irrational, beating the envoy sent by Octavian for having too long an audience with Cleopatra, only to regret his actions and write a letter of apology to his enemy. In the same chapter we see another side to Cleopatra, a woman who would do anything to calm and reassure Antony, celebrating his birthday with an opulent party. Cleopatra frequently appears as the cause of Antony's poor judgment in Josephus (*Jewish War* 1 12.5.243) as a "slave to his passion for Cleopatra." The integrity of the queen's own character is also questioned (*Jewish War* 1 8.4.359–363).

7.3 ANTONY'S OTHER WOMEN

Antony was married when he met Cleopatra, just as Julius Caesar had been. In Appian (*Civil Wars* 5.11) Cleopatra is shown to be a calming influence on Antony, who, we are told, "went out only to the temples, the schools, and the discussions of the learned, and spent his time with Greeks, out of deference to Cleopatra, to whom his sojourn in Alexandria was wholly devoted" (trans. Thackery, Loeb edition). Appian (*Civil Wars* 5.19) also mentions another dominant woman in Antony's life: Fulvia, his wife. Fulvia was politically active and, as Appian himself notes, caused considerable trouble for Mark Antony. In the second section of chapter 59 we are told of his reaction to her death: "The death of this turbulent woman, who had stirred up so disastrous a war on account of her jealousy of Cleopatra, seemed extremely fortunate to both of the parties who were rid of her. Nevertheless, Antony was much saddened by this event because he considered himself in some sense the cause of it" (trans. Thackery, Loeb edition). In chapter 66 Appian wrote that Mark Antony had a man called Manius put to death for upsetting Fulvia by mention of Antony's affair with Cleopatra. In chapter 76 Octavia, the sister of Octavian, appears, as Antony's new wife and we are told that Antony wintered with his new wife, being very much in love with her, although Appian adds that this was on account of his excessive liking of women.

In Plutarch's *Life of Antony*, Cleopatra first appears in chapter 10, where Plutarch wrote ". . . Cleopatra was indebted to Fulvia for teaching Antony to obey a wife's authority, for by the time he met her, he had already been quite broken in and schooled to accept the sway of women" (trans. Scott-Kilvert 1965). The reader does not encounter the Queen again until chapter 25, when she "enters" Mark Antony's life in the narrative. Here she is described as a "crowning mischief" at her "most beautiful." As already mentioned, the decadent lifestyle of Antony and Cleopatra forms part of Plutarch's *Life of Antony* (28). In stark contrast a reference is made to Antony's wife, Fulvia, whose fight with Octavian is mentioned. So, from the frivolous fantasy of the banquets and play-acting we are reminded of the harsh reality of war. Plutarch described, later in chapter 30, how Fulvia had lost her life, fighting for Antony's cause. In chapter 31 Antony's marriage to Octavia, sister of Octavian, is mentioned; the reader is also told that Antony did not deny his relationship with Cleopatra but did not admit that she was his wife. Later, in chapter 53, when Antony and Cleopatra's affair was in full swing, Octavia appears as a selfless and dignified counterpart to the selfishness of Cleopatra, who, we are told, was threatened by Antony's wife. We are told that Cleopatra pretended to be consumed with love for Antony in order to dissuade him from leaving her. Octavia's loyalty was such that she refused to abandon Antony and pleaded with her brother not to war against her errant husband (chapter 54). Octavia looked after Antony's children with his former wife Fulvia, and would, following their suicides, care for the children of Antony and Cleopatra.

In Suetonius' *Deified Augustus* chapter 69, Cleopatra is referred to in a series of supposed questions by Mark Antony in defense of his adultery in which he was said to have written: "what's troubling you? That I am having a go at the queen? Is she my wife? Have I just started this or has it been going on for nine years?" (Edwards 2000).

Athenaeus (*Deipnosophistai* 4.29) states that Cleopatra is said to have married Mark Antony in Cilicia. Antony is also referred to as her husband by Josephus in *Against Apion* (69). Some modern writers have suggested that the marriage took place during the festivities of the Donations of Alexandria in 34 BCE (Hölbl 2001: 244). If the marriage took place, it was not recognized by Roman law because Antony was still married to Octavia. Antony divorced Octavia in 32 BCE and, shortly afterwards, Octavian declared war (Plutarch, *Life of Antony* 57.4–5).

In Egypt, for the general population, there was no marriage ceremony, but a contract would be signed. This allowed divorces and to some extent rights for both partners. For the Greeks and particularly royals, legitimacy was a greater issue. Clearly illegitimate children had come to power, Cleopatra's father being one of them. The situation in which Cleopatra found herself was quite unique in that she, as ruler of Egypt, was the mistress. Previous extra-marital relationships had involved the (male) ruler of Egypt and his mistress. In a strange way, Cleopatra fulfilled both roles. Both Caesar and Antony had Roman wives of their own. In the case of Antony he had two – Fulvia and later

Octavia. The latter he had married after the birth of his children with Cleopatra. Whether marriage was important to Cleopatra depends largely upon where her aspirations lay. If she was concerned with preserving the Egyptian line then she had successfully done this, not with Antony or his children, but by her first-born. Some would argue that Cleopatra had even turned Caesar's death and subsequent deification to her own advantage. If, however, Cleopatra's aspirations looked beyond Egypt's borders and territories (as the Donations of Alexandria would suggest) then the legal position of her (Roman) children becomes a key policy issue.

Antony also had a male lover named Messala, an associate of Brutus, who according to Appian (*Civil Wars* 4.38) became "intimate" with Antony until the latter became the slave of Cleopatra. Not only is Cleopatra shown to have consumed Antony's interests but the abandonment of Messala is also perhaps used to illustrate Antony's abandonment of Roman traditions.

Mark Antony's position in Egypt

Mark Antony held no official role within the Egyptian ideology of kingship. Ptolemy Caesar was Cleopatra's chosen heir and Antony could not even claim to be his father. It is really overseas where the Roman general adopts the role of ruler and protector. There are few traces of Mark Antony in Egypt. One exception is the base of a statue that was found in Alexandria. The statue base makes a reference to the Association of the Inimitable Livers, as referenced in Plutarch's *Life of Antony* (28; Walker and Higgs 2001: 232). The inscription refers to a statue of Mark Antony, now missing but certainly of Greek/Roman-style, as indicated by the foot prints on top of the base, and probably made from bronze. The statue base is made from granite and the inscription is in Greek and reads "Antony, the Great Lover, lover without peer, Parasitos [set this up] to his own god and benefactor, 29th Day of Choiach, year 19." The date was December 28, 34 BCE. Parasitos is the name of the dedicant of the statue and is probably a pun referring to his parasitic status and so dependency upon Mark Antony and his money.

Antony seems to have embraced the concept of divinity, an interest that had, if the sources are believed, led to Caesar's downfall and which would ironically be accepted in the case of Octavian when he came to power as Emperor and became Augustus. Antony is said to have dressed in the guise of Dionysos during Alexandrian ceremonies.

7.4 CLEOPATRA – AMBASSADOR FOR EGYPT

Cleopatra's main foreign contact was Rome. This relationship governed many aspects of her rule, and as a consequence has dominated many biographies of the queen. There are three key areas of foreign policy during Cleopatra's reign – firstly, the Romans in Egypt; secondly, Cleopatra in Rome; and, finally, the territories and concessions awarded to Cleopatra, chiefly by Mark Antony during the second part of her rule. Syria and Cyprus in particular became key territories to Cleopatra.

A large percentage of the armed forces in Egypt during Cleopatra's reign were Roman (Chauveau 2000: 167–8). Auletes had been returned to the throne with the aid of Roman forces and in addition Caesar had left three legions in Alexandria to protect the fragile rule of the queen and the elder of her two brothers. Cleopatra's navy was still a powerful one and the queen would offer its help to Roman generals during her reign. In all respects Cleopatra had inherited a weak kingdom dependent upon outside aid to maintain order. However, her achievements, once she had sole control of the throne, were remarkable, not least because of the amount of time that she spent abroad during her reign, which would have allowed her enemies at home to gain control in her absence. It is thought that both Auletes and his daughter believed that they could rule the Mediterranean as part of a joint Romano-Ptolemaic force (Hölbl 2001: 306).

Ptolemaic possessions overseas

When Cleopatra came to the throne the Ptolemaic overseas possessions were greatly depleted. Territories had been given as gifts to illegitimate members of the family and to the Romans as a bargaining tool. So power hungry were the later rulers of the dynasty that they seem to have been willing to agree to any number of deals that potentially damaged their successors' chances of survival. Cleopatra was quite different to her immediate predecessors and managed in the second part of her rule to accumulate territories that could rival the early Ptolemaic possessions.

Cleopatra was seen as a genuine threat to Roman territory. The Roman territories under Mark Antony's control were divided into two categories, namely those which were ruled by client kings appointed by Antony, and those which were established earlier by Pompey (Walker and Higgs 2001: 233). Propertius accused Cleopatra of trying to "... spread her ... pavilions on ... Capitol hill" (*Elegies* 3.11.55–6; Slavitt 2002) in the heart of Rome and goes on to ask "what does our history mean if it leads to the rule of a woman?" (61, Slavitt 2002). Some writers, Josephus for example, imply that Cleopatra asked Antony for the territories that she gained.

Cyprus has always played a key political role in harboring exiles. The island was left to Rome in 80 BCE and in 58 BCE was finally annexed (Hölbl 2001: 226). The Romans were slow to take control of the territory. In Strabo (*Geography* 14.5.3) territories given to Cleopatra are mentioned in passing and include Amaxia, where timber was bought for ship building; a royal residence belonging to the queen; and Cyprus given by Antony to Cleopatra and her sister Arsinoe (14.6.6).

Cleopatra and her four-year-old twins were summoned to Antioch by Antony in 37 BCE (Plutarch, *Life of Antony* 36.5). It was at this time that they received their epithets Cleopatra Selene and Alexander Helios. Antony was in charge of the Eastern Roman Empire and had during the winter of 37/36 BCE made considerable additions to the Ptolemaic territories controlled by

Cleopatra (Hölbl 2001: 242–4). Cleopatra was awarded Chalkis in Lebanon following the death of its king (Porphyry 260 F 2.17), Judaea in Palestine, and neighboring Nabatea. These "gifts" greatly enhanced Ptolemaic possessions and it is now generally agreed that Antony made them not as a gesture of his affection for the queen but rather as part of his political programme in the East (Hölbl 2001: 242). The coins from this region are of considerable interest because of the way in which they present the two rulers, suggesting that Antony and Cleopatra ruled these regions as one (Hölbl 2001: 242).

Interaction with other rulers

Josephus was naturally concerned primarily with Judaea and in particular Cleopatra's interaction with Herod, who was effectively renting his country from the queen, following its gifting to her from Mark Antony. In *Jewish War* 1 12.5.243 in the context of Herod needing military support from Egypt, and in spite of Cleopatra's "magnificent" reception of the ruler, Josephus states that Herod decided to risk sailing to Rome to obtain support rather than aid the queen in return for her support (*Jewish War* 1 14.2.279). In *Jewish War* 1 8.4.359–363 we are told that "Cleopatra, after killing her own family, one after another, till not a single relative remained, was now thirsty for the blood of foreigners. Laying before Antony calumnious charges against high officials in Syria, she urged him to put them to death, in the belief that she would have no difficulty in appropriating their possessions; and her ambitions extended to Judaea and Arabia, she was secretly contriving the ruin of their respective kings, Herod and Malchus" (trans. Thackery, Loeb edition). In Josephus Cleopatra takes a very active role in his campaign of blame, not only influencing Antony but also by her own debauchery.

Josephus seems to be more interested in the political policies of Cleopatra than in her relationship with Mark Antony. The detainment of the Nabataean King Malchus is described in some detail in 14.2 (375–6). In book 15 (2.5.24) Josephus records an exchange between Cleopatra and Alexandra, wife of Alexander, son of Aristobulus. Alexandra wrote to Cleopatra, asking her to request Antony to obtain the high priesthood for her son. Mariamme, the daughter of Alexandra, was married to Herod. Alexandra was accused by Herod of plotting against him (2.7.32) by working with Cleopatra to deprive him of his power. The relationship between the two women is taken further in 15.3.2.45–46. We are told that Herod forced his wife to stay in the palace:

> She therefore wrote to Cleopatra, making a long sustained lament about the state in which she found herself and urging her to give her as much help as she possibly could. Thereupon Cleopatra told her to escape secretly with her son and come to her in Egypt. This seemed to Alexandra a good idea, and she contrived the following scheme. She had two coffins made as if for the transporting of dead bodies and placed herself and her son in them, after giving orders to those of her servants who knew the plan to take them away during the night. From there they had a road to the sea and a ship ready for them to sail in to Egypt. But her servant Aesop incautiously reported this to Sabbion, one of her friends, thinking that he knew the plan. Alexandra was caught in the act of escaping. (3.2.48)

The parallel with Cleopatra's earlier meeting with Caesar, when she was hidden in order to enter the royal palaces, is perhaps notable. Herod "overlooked Alexandra's offence because he did not dare take any harsh measures against her, even though he would have liked to, for Cleopatra, out of hatred toward him, would not have allowed her to be accused." The reason for this story is Josephus can show that Herod "made a show of magnanimity" in dealing with the situation.

In book 15 (3.5.62–65) further meddling by Cleopatra is recorded. Josephus, contrary to the other historical sources, records that

> Alexandra wrote to Cleopatra about Herod's plot and the killing of her son. Since she (Cleopatra) had long been eager to come

> to the help of Alexandra in answer to her pleas, and pitied her ill fortune, Cleopatra made the whole matter her own concern, and did not cease urging Antony to avenge the murder of Alexandra's son, for, she said, it was not right that Herod, who had been appointed by him as king of a country which he had no claim to rule, should have exhibited such lawlessness towards those who were the real kings.

It has been suggested that Cleopatra's intervention took place in 35–34 BCE, when Antony was in Egypt. Further victimization of Herod by Cleopatra is referred to in book 15 (3.8.75–77), when the queen was apparently chastised by Antony for meddling in Herod's affairs. Josephus notes that Egypt's interest in Herod was purely on the grounds of obtaining Judaea as a territory. The queen's greed is mentioned again in 3.8.79, where we are told Antony gave her Coele Syria.

Josephus also held Cleopatra responsible for the wars between Herod and the Nabataean King Malchus (5.1.110 and 5.3.131–32) for her own benefit and a means of gaining more territories. The queen's culpability is also referred to in 6.6.191 when Antony was told that the only way to save himself and his power was to get rid of Cleopatra. Following the downfall of Cleopatra and Antony, we are told that the aforementioned Mariamme was only saved from death by Herod on account of their defeat (7.3.215). Herod himself also gained 400 Gauls who had been Cleopatra's bodyguards plus territorial gains (7.3.217). In book 15 (2.6.28) there is also a reference to Antony's *paidika* (lover or favorite) Quintus Dellius (also in Josephus, *Jewish Antiquities* 14.394 and *Jewish War* 1.290), who abandoned him for Octavian before the battle of Actium. Dellius later wrote a history of Antony's Parthian campaigns, which is mentioned in Horace (Ode 2.3).

Later in book 15 (7.9.256–58) a retrospective comment is made regarding Salome (Herod's sister) who was married to the governor of Idumaea and who was another prominent woman who was clearly seen to meddle in international affairs. Salome asked for control of her home territory, offering the state's allegiance to the queen. We are told that Cleopatra asked Antony for the territory but was refused.

In *Civil Wars* (4.61) Appian details the actions of Cassius, who asked Cleopatra and Serapio (her viceroy in Cyprus) for help. We are told that the queen refused help on account of Egypt suffering famine, but Appian adds that the real reason was because she was co-operating with Dolabella and had sent him legions and a fleet. Cleopatra had sent her fleet to aid Octavian and Antony against Cassius, and we are told that the latter believed Egypt to be in a weak state on account of the famine and that the Romans legions had left. The reasons given for Cleopatra's support of Octavian and Antony were her relationship with Caesar (whose name they defended) and also on account of her fear of Cassius, thus illustrating two emotions that might have been seen to be typical of a woman. Appian's *Civil Wars* (4.82) also records that the fleet was damaged by a storm on the Libyan coast and also that Cleopatra returned home in ill-health.

7.5 THE VICTORY PARADE OF THE ARMENIAN KING AND DONATIONS OF ALEXANDRIA

Following two difficult years of campaigns against Parthia and then Armenia, Antony was finally victorious. Antony brought the conquered king of Armenia to Alexandria and presented him to Cleopatra (Josephus, *Jewish Antiquities* 15 4.3.104). For this procession Antony dressed as Dionysos, a clear reference to Ptolemy XII who presented himself as the New Dionysos. A number of writers refer to this event, which took place in the temple of Sarapis. Cleopatra received her guests seated on a golden throne (Plutarch, *Life of Antony* 50; Dio XLIX.41.1). A second ceremony then took place, an event which has become known as the Donations of Alexandria. On this occasion the venue was the more public space of the gymnasium. In Plutarch's version (*Life of Antony* 50) the reader is told that the defeated king of Armenia was sent to Alexandria for the benefit of Cleopatra and Egypt, thus illustrating how Cleopatra's influence was causing a much wider effect.

The Donations of Alexandria have already been mentioned with regard to Cleopatra as the goddess Isis. Two accounts of the event survive in Plutarch's *Life of Antony* 54.5–9 and Dio's *Roman History* 49.40.2–41.4 (Jones 2006: 115–17). The ceremony followed Antony's victorious campaign in Armenia and is used by the Roman authors to illustrate Mark Antony's increasingly "oriental" behavior in that this was not the usual Roman way in which to celebrate a military victory. Most of all, the passages prove Antony's lack of affinity to Rome. Plutarch even says as much in his comment on the ceremony.

According to Plutarch the main ceremony took place in the gymnasium, where a silver platform with two gold thrones for Cleopatra and Antony, and smaller thrones for the children, were set up. Antony declared Cleopatra queen of Egypt, Cyprus, Libya, and Central Syria, and Ptolemy XV as her co-ruler. Alexander Helios was given Armenia, Media, and Parthia. Ptolemy Philadelphos was awarded Phoenicia, Syria, and Cilicia. Plutarch also says that Antony's two sons took the title King of Kings. The Ptolemies were dressed appropriately for the occasion – Cleopatra as Isis and with the title New Isis, Alexander Helios with a Median headdress, and Ptolemy Philadelphos with soldier's boots, a cloak, woollen hat, and crown as a reference to his Macedonian ancestors. Cleopatra Selene is not mentioned here. The passage reads as follows (53):

> For after filling the gymnasium with a throng and placing on a tribunal of silver two thrones of gold, one for himself and the other for Cleopatra, and other lower thrones for his sons, in the first place he declared Cleopatra Queen of Egypt, Cyprus, Libya, and Coele Syria, and she was to share her throne with Ptolemy Caesar. Ptolemy Caesar was believed to be a son of the former Caesar, by whom Cleopatra was left pregnant. In the second place, he proclaimed his own sons by Cleopatra Kings of Kings, and to Alexander he allotted Armenia, Media and Parthia (when he should have subdued it), to Ptolemy Phoenicia, Syria, and Cilicia. At the same time he also produced his sons, Alexander arrayed in Median garb, which included a tiara and upright head-dress, Ptolemy in boots, short cloak, and broad-brimmed hat

> surmounted by a diadem. For the latter was the dress of the kings who followed Alexander, the former that of Medes and Armenians. And when the boys had embraced their parents, one was given a bodyguard of Armenians, the other of Macedonians. (trans. Thayer, Loeb edition)

In Dio's account we are told that the Armenian king and his family were brought to Cleopatra, who was seated on a silver platform with gold throne. Following this presentation Antony held a banquet for the Alexandrians and Cleopatra and her children sat with him. In an address he proclaimed Cleopatra as Queen of Kings, and Ptolemy XV as King of Kings. He granted Cleopatra and her son Egypt and Cyprus. The youngest child, Ptolemy Philadelphos, was given Syria and all of the lands of the Euphrates Valley as far as the Hellespont; Cleopatra Selene was given Libya and Cyrenaica; and finally Alexander Helios, her twin, was given Armenia and the lands along the Euphrates as far as India.

The problem was, as Dio points out, that these lands were not Mark Antony's to give. Some scholars have suggested that the Donations of Alexandria were merely a spectacle and that in reality no territories were gained (Chauveau 2002: 60). However, there are some features within the historical text that are worthy of further consideration. The Roman Senate was outraged by news of the Donations (Plutarch, *Life of Antony* 55), and the level of detail of the contents of the ceremony seems to have been used here to stress its ostentatious nature.

In Plutarch's version the children, including Ptolemy XV, sat on smaller thrones below those of Cleopatra and Antony. In Dio's version Cleopatra is distinguished from the others by sitting on a throne. If the accounts are accurate Cleopatra is adopting a role that is quite different from that found on the Egyptian temple reliefs that feature Ptolemy XV. At Denderah the young ruler dominates the scenes both in his position when accompanied by his mother and also in that he usually appears alone on the inside walls. Dio records that the titles of Queen of Kings and King of Kings were awarded to the queen and her son, which is more in line with the presentation that we find in the temples. However, Plutarch recorded the title of King of Kings as going only to Mark Antony's sons. I would expect Cleopatra Selene to have been awarded some of the territories, as in Dio's account, but this would be unprecedented, even by Ptolemaic standards. In ancient societies women should of course marry and would move to their new husband's country. Things may have been different if Ptolemy Caesar had been a girl and perhaps then Cleopatra would have ruled with her daughter. It would have been an interesting problem to solve. Antony's role in the whole spectacle was one of a foreign head of state. Nowhere in the literary sources does it suggest that he ruled Egypt, and in fact his actions, according to Dio, were in the name of Julius Caesar.

It has been suggested that there are two surviving representations of Alexander Helios in Eastern dress (Walker and Higgs 2001: 250–1, no. 270). The figures show a youngish male child with a full, rounded face that has been likened to the portraits of the Emperor Nero (Hermann 1988: 288–93), but are not dissimilar to the images of Ptolemy VIII, particularly with regard to the rendering of the chubby face, rounded fleshy chin, and the closely-set eyes. The figures are substantial for images made in copper alloy; one example, now housed in the Metropolitan Museum stands at 64 centimeters. The child wears two distinctive attributes: a pyramidal-shaped headdress and long trousers in a style that is typical of those worn by Persians in Greek art. There is nothing specific, however, by which to identify this image as a representation of Alexander Helios in his Eastern costume at the ceremony.

Josephus (*Jewish Antiquities* 15 4.1.88–95) states that Antony gave Cleopatra the cities between the Eleutherus River and Egypt with the exception of Tyre and Sidon, which he knew to have been free from the time of their ancestors, although "she earnestly pleaded that they be given to her" (trans. Thackery, Loeb edition). In 4.4.106 Herod is again recorded paying his tribute to Cleopatra from whom he had to rent his own land. The mention of it being unsafe for him not to do so refers not only to the queen's power but to her supporter Antony and so the Romans.

7.6 COINS OF CLEOPATRA AND OF ANTONY AND CLEOPATRA OVERSEAS

A number of coins were minted to celebrate Cleopatra's newly acquired territories. On some examples Cleopatra and Antony appear together, the queen on the obverse and the Roman general on the reverse.

Some of the coins minted in Chalcis, one of the territories awarded to Cleopatra by Mark Antony, showed Cleopatra's bust on the obverse and Antony's on the reverse. In other issues Antony was replaced by an established god (Walker and Higgs 2001: 233, nos. 214–17). The coins, which were minted between 32/31 BCE, were produced in Cleopatra's name and the legends read "of Queen Cleopatra." Cleopatra appears as a ruler; her hair is styled in the usual melon coiffure and she wears a diadem. Mark Antony's image is restricted to the head and neck. The two "portraits" are similar, with an emphasis on a strong profile, and a large eye, no doubt a reference to the Herakleian line with whom they were in different ways connected (Walker and Higgs 2001: 236).

The Antioch mint reveals further developments in the two rulers' "portrait" types (Walker 2003b). Once again Antony and Cleopatra appear individually on coins from this region, but also appear together. On silver tetradrachms, minted between 37–32 BCE, Cleopatra appears on the obverse with the legend "Queen Cleopatra Thea II." The term *thea*, Greek for goddess, is also a reference to one of Cleopatra's ancestors – Cleopatra Thea. Antony appears on the reverse with the legend "Antony, Imperator for third time and Triumvir." The representations are the same as those on the Chalcis coins; Cleopatra appears in the form of a bust, here wearing an elaborate dress and necklace, and Antony is shown only to the base of his neck. Both rulers appeared on coins from Antioch independently of one another (Walker and Higgs 2001: 234, nos. 218–22). The same portraits and dress, in the case of Cleopatra, are found on coins from an unknown mint in the form of silver denarii (Walker 2003: 509–10). Cleopatra's appears with the Latin rather than the usual

Greek legend "Queen of kings and her children who are of kings." Antony celebrates his victory over Armenia on the obverse with the legend *M. Antoni Armenia devicta*. It has been suggested that the denarii were directly associated with the commemoration of the Donations of Alexandria (Walker 2003b: 510).

Bronze coins showing the royal pair, as usual Cleopatra on the obverse and Antony on the reverse, were also minted at Ptolemais Ake (Walker and Higgs 2001: 235, no. 231). In 34/33 BCE the city of Dora, along the coast to the south of Ptolemais, minted coins showing the rulers in jugate (side by side on a single side).

The adoption of eastern dress by Cleopatra on a number of these coins perhaps mimics the dressing up in the pageant of the actual Donations ceremony. Antony and Cleopatra were not the first to engage in such acculturation. Alexander had been known to dress in the costumes of those he conquered and Cleopatra's own family had clearly adopted their Egyptian roles enthusiastically.

It is the "portrait" used by Cleopatra on such coins that has prompted many to make reference to her large hooked nose and pointed chin. These features mimicked the presentation of the queen's father, Ptolemy XII, and seem in turn to have been adopted by Mark Antony.

Coinage showing Cleopatra alone

A mint often identified as Damascus, but in fact uncertain, produced coins representing Cleopatra (Walker and Higgs 2001: 235, nos. 223–4, and 230). If these coins were struck at Damascus they were in honor of Cleopatra because strictly speaking the city was not a Ptolemaic territory (Walker 2003b: 510–11; Walker and Higgs 2001: 235, no. 230). The coin portrait shows the queen with the usual diadem, perhaps a little thinner on the example in the aforementioned catalogue (Walker and Higgs 2001) than was typical. This type was issued in 37/36 BCE and 33/32 BCE, and so are towards the end of Cleopatra's reign. This image of the queen includes an elaborate necklace and is in the form of a bust rather than a head.

Bronze coins were also minted and dated by a different regnal year of Cleopatra in Phoenicia, which began in 37/36 BCE, for example Orthosia (Walker and Higgs 2001: 235, nos. 225–6), Tripolis (Walker and Higgs 2001: 235, no. 227), and Berytus (Walker and Higgs 2001: 235, nos. 228–9). These portraits show the head and neck only; the queen wears the usual diadem, with her hair pulled back into a melon coiffure. There is a variety of portraits, but on the majority the chin and nose are prominent in the manner of Ptolemy XII's portrait type. On some examples earrings are clearly visible.

7.7 ACTIUM AND POST-ACTIUM

There were a number of reasons for Octavian's declaration of war against Cleopatra: the divorce of his sister, the territories that rightly belonged to Rome being given to Cleopatra, and the blatant manner in which Antony celebrated his link to the queen, as for instance on coinage.

During what would be the final years of their rule, Cleopatra and Antony spent a considerable amount of time outside Egypt (Hölbl 2001: 244–7). At the start of 32 BCE the pair were stationed at Ephesus, by April of that year they were on the island of Samos, and in May or June they visited Athens. By the winter of 32/1 BCE Antony and Cleopatra moved to Patras and it was in the following spring that war broke out, ending on September 2, 31 BCE with the battle of Actium, on the west coast of Greece.

In Plutarch's *Life of Antony* throughout the preparation for battle (60) Cleopatra is shown not to take matters seriously and in chapter 63 she is blamed for the fatal decision to fight Octavian at sea rather than on land, where Antony would have been stronger. Cleopatra does not really appear in the battle descriptions, except towards the end in chapter 66 when she turned her ships and left; Mark Antony famously followed Cleopatra and thus the pair were defeated by Octavian and the Roman fleet. According to Plutarch, following the battle of Actium and after a brief period of depression (67 and 69), the pair returned to Alexandria and their licentious lifestyle. The Association of "Inimitable Livers" was disbanded and the "Order of the Inseparable in Death" was inaugurated and, in another display of her acceptance of the situation, we are told that Cleopatra started to collect venomous creatures and to test poisons on prisoners (71).

Dio (1) starts with the naval battle on September 2. Following the flight of Antony and Cleopatra we are told that Octavian sent chase but in realizing that he would not catch the fugitives, he turned his attention to the remaining supporters and boats, who surrendered without fight. In chapter 6 Antony and Cleopatra are not shown as depressed hostages but we are told they made preparations for war. Dio reveals that their fall-back plan was to sail to Spain and to stir up a revolt there or to move to the Red Sea and to wage war upon Rome from there. Cleopatra is then shown to be the more devious of the two. We are told that she sent Octavian a scepter and crown to signify that she offered him her kingdom. Dio states that she hoped he would take pity on her (presumably being a woman). We are then told that Octavian, after accepting the gifts, offered her a deal in which if she killed Antony he would grant her a pardon and leave her to rule Egypt.

Dio (7) also catalogues the supposed allies who abandoned Antony and Cleopatra and those who remained faithful to their patrons. The desperation of both Antony and Cleopatra is described in chapter 8, where we are told they sent envoys reminding Octavian of their friendship and offering great wealth respectively. From Antony's son Antyllus Octavian accepted gifts but sent nothing in return. While to Cleopatra, we are told, "he sent many threats and promises alike." Dio claims that Cleopatra had "collected all of her wealth in her tomb, which was being contructed in the royal grounds, and she threatened to burn it all up with her in case she should fail of even the slightest of her demands." Realizing that he himself was not the best person to negotiate with the queen, whose irrational nature is implied by this section of text, we are told that Octavian sent a freedman named Thyrsus to negotiate. Dio also claims that Thyrsus was to tell the queen that "(Octavian) was in love with her" in the hope that she would abandon Antony because "she thought it her due to be loved by all mankind."

Following a brief interlude on Antony's movements, Dio returns to Cleopatra and Octavian, recording the latter's conquest of Pelusium, which was taken "ostensibly by storm, but really because it was betrayed by Cleopatra." The main reason for her abandonment of Pelusium was given to be that the queen believed Octavian was in love with her. Dio goes on to suggest that when Octavian entered Alexandria the queen prevented the Alexandrians from attacking him, on account that "she expected to gain not only forgiveness and the sovereignty over the Egyptians, but the empire of the Romans as well."

Mark Antony, on the other hand, is said (10) to have attempted to prevent Octavian taking Alexandria both through force and bribery, by firing leaflets into Octavian's camp offering rewards for those who abandoned it. Antony was defeated on land and in his attempts to bribe Octavian's men, and so turned to his fleet, we are told, with the intention of either preparing for a second sea battle or in order to flee to Spain. Cleopatra's repsonse is said to have been to disband the fleet, suggesting a lack of unity between the two lovers. At this point Cleopatra locked herself in her mausoleum. Dio's interpretation of Cleopatra's abandonment of Antony is that she hoped he would join her. In a psychological analysis Dio says that Cleopatra hoped that Antony, upon hearing of her death, would end his own life.

Dio (15) records that the Alexandrians and Egyptians who supported Cleopatra were spared by Octavian. Dio goes on to record that, following Egypt's capture, we are told

> it rained not only water where no drop had ever fallen previously, but also blood; and there were flashes of armor from the clouds as this bloody rain fell from them. Elsewhere there was the clashing of drums and cymbals and the notes of flutes and trumpets,

> and a serpent of huge size suddenly appeared to them and uttered an incredibly loud hiss. Meanwhile comets were seen and dead men's ghosts appeared, the statues frowned, and Apis bellowed a note of lamentation and burst into tears. (trans. Thayer, Loeb edition)

Cleopatra, we are told, had taken all offerings from "even the holiest shrines," an idea that was also promoted by Josephus.

Josephus' *Jewish War* 20.1.389–391, 20.3.396–397, and 22.3.440 contain references to Cleopatra following the battle of Actium. In 20.1 Herod is recorded as having said

> When no longer useful as an ally (after the battle of Actium), I (Herod) became his [Mark Antony's] best counsellor; I told him the one remedy for his disasters – the death of Cleopatra. Would he but kill her, I promised him money, walls to protect him, an army, and myself as his brother in arms in the war against you (Octavian). But his ears it seems were stopped by his infatuation for Cleopatra and by god who has granted you the mastery. (trans. Thayer, Loeb edition)

It is clear that Josephus, through his record of Herod's actions, followed the formal Roman party line of accrediting Cleopatra with blame rather than Antony as the gullible Roman general.

There is also a fragmentary Latin papyrus that includes passages on the events following the battle of Actium, discussed (in Latin) by Garuti (1958). The small fragments describe the flight of Cleopatra following the battle of Actium (1958: 51–6), Cornelius Gallus, poet and first prefect of Egypt (56–8), Cleopatra and Mark Antony (58–61), and Cornelius Gallus and the Roman legions (61–7). The columns also cover the period following Octavian's landing at Pelusium (70–6), and the planned deaths of Antony and Cleopatra (81–6) as the desperation of the situation became clear.

A marble relief, possibly depicting a Roman warship from the battle of Actium, was found at a necropolis at Praeneste. This small town is today called Palestrina and is on the far outskirts of Rome. It is famous for its large Nilotic mosaic, which formed part of the main Roman sanctuary's decorative scheme (Meyboom 1995; Walker 2003c). Today the marble relief with warship is housed in the Vatican Museums (Walker and Higgs 2001: 262–3, no. 311). The block originally belonged to a frieze and shows a bireme (double set of oars) battleship with 11 men on board. These figures are carved in varying levels of relief allowing a three-dimensional presentation of the group. At the side of the relief a soldier on horseback appears. A seventeenth-century drawing of the same relief suggests that it came from a Roman Republican cemetery, in which case it was probably originally part of a funerary monument (Walker and Higgs 2001: 262). The link to Egypt and the battle of Actium is on account of the crocodile beside the prow of the ship. It has been suggested that the owner of the funerary monument may have been one of Antony's soldiers in Egypt at this time. A connection between the Palestrina mosaic and Cleopatra and Mark Antony has also been suggested (Walker 2003).

8

DEATH OF A QUEEN, REBIRTH OF A GODDESS

8.1 WRITTEN SOURCES

Speculation surrounded Cleopatra's death immediately after the event. The ancient accounts concentrate on the manner of her suicide, most notably on whether she poisoned herself or was bitten by an asp. It is recorded by Plutarch (*Life of Antony* 86) that in the absence of the living queen for the victory parade in Rome, Octavian included a statue of the queen with an asp. The Greek adverb used here is usually translated as "clinging firmly." To what extent this statue has become part of the mythology is worth considering, particularly since the reference only appears several years after the event. It seems possible, given the lack of understanding by the Romans of Egyptian iconography during the first century BC, that the snake may simply have been the uraeus of an Egyptian-style statue and that the asp was the uraeus on the brow of a statue, not necessarily a representation of Cleopatra but as one of any Egyptian queen wearing the royal cobra. The true source of the statue with cobra story is of course impossible to determine with any accuracy. The plausibility of a two-meter cobra being smuggled into the mausoleum has been questioned by modern historians. It has also been suggested that the statue itself was behind the theory of death by snake bite. The early writers Strabo, Virgil, Propertius, and Horace all suggest that Cleopatra committed suicide by means of the poisonous bite of a snake (Whitehorne 1994: 191–2). And so the argument becomes circular. It is of course possible that the rumor surrounding the means of suicide was entirely separate from the reference to a statue. Problems in determining the accuracy of such reports are simply part of the Cleopatra mythology. It does sometimes pay to question rather than simply accept or justify references that conveniently support the common thread of a historical narrative.

In some respects Horace offers a tabloid account of the death of Cleopatra. It is based on contemporary information that must have circulated around certain sections of Roman society and its aim was clearly to honor and promote Octavian, now Augustus, the patron of this group of poets and the very man who had saved the situation; who, as Horace wrote, "saw to it that she was restored from madness to a state of realistic terror" – who in today's terms forced her to "get a grip." The Cleopatra in Horace is a hysterical woman, who redeemed herself only to save herself from further embarrassment. It has never been easy to be a woman in a man's world and it seems fair to conclude that Cleopatra's reputation suffered on account of her relationship with Antony, whose conduct contemporary writers seem to have criticized, irrespective of his relationship with the queen. We thus find Cleopatra implicated in the corruption of Mark Antony and his own weakness in following the queen is a common theme in the written sources. At the end of Horace's ode is an explanation for Cleopatra's suicide and one that has been quoted by many of her biographers: that Cleopatra did not wish to be captured and displayed in Rome as a trophy of war.

In Propertius' *Elegies* 3.11 poetic licence prevails to describe how Cleopatra was shackled and paraded in Rome with the marks of the snakebites visible on her arms (Slavitt 2002: 67–70). In fact a statue of the queen is referred to in other sources. Writing shortly after her death, in book 17.1.10, Strabo refers to the two theories surrounding the event, writing that the queen came into Octavian's power alive but soon after took her own life by either "the bite of an asp or by applying poisonous ointment" (trans. Thayer, Loeb edition). Cleopatra's cunning is a common theme within historical accounts of her death. Velleius Paterculus (2:87), for example, wrote "Cleopatra, baffling the vigilance of her guards she caused an asp to be smuggled in to her, and ended her life by its venomous sting untouched by a woman's fears" (trans. Thayer, Loeb edition).

It is only really in the later writings of Plutarch and Cassius Dio that the death of Cleopatra is discussed in any real detail. Both authors wrote long after the event and both accounts contain sections that are highly conjectural. Plutarch's account is also simply a section in the biography of Mark Antony.

Death of Antony

The reader is told that, after their defeat at the battle of Actium and the subsequent desertion by their army, Cleopatra fled to her mausoleum (76) and "let down the hanging doors which were strengthened with bars and bolts and sent messengers to tell Antony that she was dead." In a supposed quote Antony laments that Cleopatra was braver than he in that she committed suicide, thus taking the honorable option; even his slave Eros was able to take his own life, leaving Antony to make a failed attempt on his own. The wounded Antony was taken to Cleopatra's monument. The building is thought to have been on two levels or raised because when the queen would not open the doors, Antony was lifted in (see also Dio). Plutarch makes much of the "pitiable sight" of the wounded Roman ruler being hoisted up to Cleopatra. Once again Cleopatra's strength is referred to as she struggled to pull Antony towards her. Plutarch wrote in considerable detail, as if he had witnessed the incident with his own eyes:

> The task was almost beyond a woman's strength, and it was only with great difficultly that Cleopatra, clinging with both hands to the rope and with the muscles of her face distorted by the strain, was able to haul him up, whilst those on the ground encouraged her with their cries and shared her agony.

The actual death of Antony is described (77) – he died from his wounds.

Plutarch also informs the reader of Antony's wishes (58), stating that he declared in his will that his body should be sent to Cleopatra in Egypt, most likely presuming he would die in battle overseas. Antony's banqueting, reading of love letters in public, and gifts to Cleopatra were all criticized by the Romans. Even the aforementioned Dellius (Antony's young favorite) was said to be in fear of his life (59).

Cleopatra and Octavian

Octavian said that he would grant Cleopatra anything within reason on condition that she put Antony to death or expel him from Egypt. Octavian's landing at the city of Pelusium and its subsequent surrender marked the start of Roman occupation (Plutarch, *Life of Antony* 74). The reader is also told that Cleopatra had built "a number of high monuments and tombs of great beauty near the temple of Isis," and that she collected her treasures together. Following this chapter, Plutarch concentrates on the death of the queen (see below).

Moving on from the death of Antony, Plutarch continues his *Life of Antony* by considering the subsequent relationship between Cleopatra and Octavian (78). Plutarch states that the Roman general feared that Cleopatra might set fire to her treasure and that he wanted to capture her so that the queen could take part in his victory parade in Rome. No doubt Cleopatra realized her fate. We are told that her only request to Octavian was a reiteration of part of her original appeal for her children be allowed to succeed her and take charge of her kingdom. This accords with her presentation of Ptolemy Caesar as her co-ruler and heir. In chapter 83 Cleopatra and Octavian meet in person. Plutarch's description of her physical appearance includes an aside that, despite her sorry state, her charm and beauty were still apparent. There is an additional account of Cleopatra's feisty character. On discovering that one of her stewards had told Octavian she was concealing a considerable number of her treasures the queen leapt to her feet, seized him by the hair and pummelled his face.

Cleopatra's ability to fool, and so one might assume charm, Octavian is also revealed in this passage. Cleopatra claimed that the treasures she had set aside were gifts for Octavia and Livia (the sister and wife of Octavian), and the Roman general, we are told, took this act as a positive sign that Cleopatra wished to live.

Cleopatra's suicide

Plutarch (chapter 60) portrays a woman who had accepted her own fate but who seems to deny the most likely outcome for her lover and her heir. Cleopatra was said to have asked for her children to remain on the throne in Egypt and for Antony to retire to Athens, should he not be allowed to remain (Plutarch, *Life of Antony* 72). She was refused her request (73).

Plutarch (79) then mentions the first of Cleopatra's suicide attempts, when two of Octavian's men try to distract her and attempt to scale the building. The queen tried to stab herself but was prevented from doing so by Proculeius, one of Octavian's men, who then checked for poison. A second suicide attempt, by starvation, was made following the burial of Mark Antony's body (82). In chapters 84 and 85 Antony is cremated and Cleopatra tends to his interment, planning her own death.

As follows chapter 85 records with the death of Cleopatra. Plutarch writes:

> So Cleopatra mourned Antony, and she crowned his urn with a garland and kissed it. Then she ordered a bath to be made ready, and, when she had come from the bath, she lay down and was served with an exquisite meal. Presently, there arrived an Egyptian peasant carrying a basket, and when the guards asked him what was in it, he stripped away the leaves at the top and showed them that it was full of figs. The guards were astonished at the size and beauty of the figs, whereupon the man smiled and invited them to take some, and in this way their suspicions were lulled and they allowed him to bring his fruit to the queen. When Cleopatra had dined, she took a tablet on which she had already written

> and put her seal, and sent this to Octavian Caesar. Soon afterwards she dismissed all her attendants except for two faithful waiting women, and closed the doors of the monument.

Octavian tried to revive the queen upon receiving her message, but failed. We are told that when his guards opened the tomb they found Cleopatra in her royal robes and her two attendants Iras and Charmian dying. Chapter 86 contains Plutarch's analysis of the stories surrounding the death of Cleopatra. Two alternative accounts are given: the first that a snake was concealed under the leaves of the fig basket and upon moving the figs Cleopatra allowed it to bite her arm. A second version states that the snake was brought in a vessel and that the queen provoked it by pricking it with a golden spindle until it attacked her arm. The third version of the story seems to be the most probable – that Cleopatra carried a hollow comb in her hair in which poison was stored. Plutarch is clearly confused; he states that no asp was found nor did the queen show any of the usual signs of reacting to poison. He does comment that some people recorded seeing punctures on her arm. Octavian seems to have supported the snake theory for, in place of the queen in his victory procession, he exhibited a statue of her with an asp. Cleopatra was buried alongside Antony and we are told that her body was laid beside his. Her statues were rescued by one of her friends, Archibius, who paid Octavian 2,000 talents to save them. It has been suggested that these statues were Egyptian and have survived (Walker and Higgs 2001).

Suetonius also discusses Cleopatra's death, albeit briefly, in *Deified Augustus* (17). The reader is told that Augustus "greatly desired to lead Cleopatra as a captive in his triumphal procession and even had *Psylli* [Africans who were known for their handling of snakes] brought to her who were to suck out the venomous liquid from her snake bites." We are told that Augustus honored the queen and Mark Antony by allowing the tomb she had part-built to be completed and for the pair to be buried together there.

Like Plutarch, Dio wrote a lengthy discussion on the death of Cleopatra (10 onwards), and much of the account is comparable to that of Plutarch in his *Life of Antony*. The narrative starts with Cleopatra fleeing to her tomb with a eunuch and two maidservants. As in Plutarch she sent a message to Mark Antony to say that she was dead. According to Dio Antony asked onlookers to slay him, but his companion killed himself. Antony wished to imitate his courage and thrust his sword into himself, and fell to the ground. The remaining bystanders believed that he was dead. A more detailed impression of the tomb in which Cleopatra was locked is given at this point. We are told that the doors were sealed but that the upper part next to the roof was not at this time completed. "Antony was carried to the monument and pulled up to the top of the building by the ropes that were hanging there to lift the stone blocks. Antony died there in Cleopatra's arms" (trans. Thayer, Loeb edition).

In chapter 11, with Antony dead, Cleopatra was able to turn her attention and, if Dio is to be believed, her affection towards Octavian. Cleopatra is said to have confided in Octavian, but did not trust him fully. Dio says that the queen remained in her mausoleum with "fire to consume her wealth" and an assortment of "asps and other reptiles to destroy herself, and she had the latter tried on human beings, to see in what way they killed in each case." Her aim was to purchase a pardon and to maintain Egypt. This accords with Plutarch's version of events.

Dio, like Plutarch, states that Octavian was keen to seize Cleopatra alive so that she might be paraded in a triumphal procession. It is generally accepted by both ancient and modern historians that it was a fear of this that caused Cleopatra to commit suicide. Following the failed first attempt, Octavian sent a second freedman to Cleopatra, Gaius Proculeius, who seized the queen part way though their meeting and took away the aforementioned means by which she might have harmed herself and also have destroyed her treasures. Cleopatra was then left to embalm Antony's body and subsequently taken from the mausoleum to the royal palaces. The queen then asked for an audience with Octavian.

Chapter 12 details the meeting between Cleopatra and Octavian, with Dio elaborating upon Cleopatra's attempted seduction of the Roman. Here Cleopatra is without doubt an object of male fantasy (see chapter 1): "She (Cleopatra) accordingly prepared a splendid apartment and a costly couch, and moreover arrayed herself with affected negligence, indeed, her mourning garb wonderfully became her, and seated herself upon the couch." Dio says that Cleopatra surrounded herself with images of Julius Caesar, and held his letters. When Augustus entered Dio claims that Cleopatra offered Caesar's letters in order to attempt to seduce her enemy. Dio writes:

> After she had spoken thus, she proceeded to read many passionate expressions of Caesar's. And now she would lament and kiss the letters, and again she would fall before his images and do them reverence. She kept turning her eyes towards Caesar and bewailing her fate in musical accents. She spoke in melting tones, saying at one time, "Of what avail to me, Caesar, are these thy letters?" and at anyone, "But in this man here thou also art alive for me"; again, "Would that I had died before thee," and still again, "But if I have him, I have thee." Such were the subtleties of speech and of attitude which she employed, and sweet were the glances she cast at him and the words she murmured to him. (trans. Thayer, Loeb edition)

We are told that Octavian showed no emotion towards his captive and that in desperation Cleopatra threw herself at his feet and wept. Here Cleopatra is shown to be of weak character (she was a woman after all). Defeated, Cleopatra asked to be permitted to be buried with Antony. Octavian of course, as the reader is aware, wished to keep Cleopatra alive (13) and, perhaps realizing this, Cleopatra is said to have changed tactics and pretended not to wish to die. The death itself is only awarded a short paragraph by Dio:

> First she gave a sealed paper, in which she begged Caesar to order that she be buried beside Antony, to Epaphroditus himself to deliver, pretending that it contained some other matter, and then, having by this excuse freed herself of his presence, she set about her task. She put on her most beautiful apparel, arranged her body

in most seemly fashion, took in her hands all the emblems of royalty, and so died. (trans. Thayer, Loeb edition)

In chapter 14 Dio allows himself to consider the speculation surrounding Cleopatra's death, turning into an early version of a super sleuth. It seems that Dio has little real evidence to support his speculations, which is possibly why it is separated from the brief description of Cleopatra's death. Dio writes:

> No one knows clearly in what way she perished, for the only marks on her body were slight pricks on the arm. Some say she applied to herself an asp which had been brought in to her in a water-jar, or perhaps hidden in some flowers. Others declare that she had smeared a pin, with which she was wont to fasten her hair, with some poison possessed of such a property that in ordinary circumstances it would not injure the body at all, but if it came into contact with even a drop of blood would destroy the body very quietly and painlessly; and that previous to this time she had worn it in her hair as usual, but now had made a slight scratch on her arm and had dipped the pin in the blood. In this or in some very similar way she perished, and her two handmaidens with her. As for the eunuch, he had of his own accord delivered himself up to the serpents at the very time of Cleopatra's arrest, and after being bitten by them had leaped into a coffin already prepared for him. (trans. Thayer, Loeb edition)

Octavian, we are told, was shocked at the news of Cleopatra's suicide. Dio also refers to the Psylli, mentioned by Suetonius, who attempted to revive the queen. Although Dio states that Cleopatra kept reptiles with a view to suicide, he only states that the eunuch killed himself by snake bite (Baldwin 1964: 182). However, the fact that two authors claim Augustus tried to resuscitate Cleopatra by using the talents of the Psylli suggests that he believed she had used snake poison as a means of suicide (Baldwin 1964: 182), although whether this part of the story was used simply to illustrate his attempts to keep the queen alive is not known. Two authors' accounts do not necessarily mean that their work is accurate, but rather that they used the same earlier written source for their work.

Octavian, in failing to resuscitate Cleopatra, "felt both admiration and pity for her, and was excessively grieved on his own account, as if he had been deprived of all the glory of his victory." Chapter 15 continues Dio's character analysis of the pair who "had caused many evils to the Egyptians and many to the Romans, made war and met their death in the manner I have described." We are told that the couple were embalmed and buried in the same tomb.

Few authors question the validity of the circumstances surrounding Cleopatra's death, preferring to repeat the tidy narrative of the queen's last few days. In 1925 Spiegelberg argued that not only had Cleopatra VII died by snake bite but that the associated symbolism had been intentional and the method of death specifically selected. The symbolism to which Spiegelberg referred was the royal cobra that protects rulers and some gods. Griffiths (1961: 113–18) discussed the hypothesis and quite rightly questioned the idea that a symbol intended to protect a ruler would be turned against its charge. Griffiths also correctly questioned another theory by Spiegelberg that suggested the snake was associated with the goddess Isis. This affiliation was, as Griffiths deduced, a later Roman development and there is no evidence from the Ptolemaic period to suggest that Isis was accompanied by a cobra, with the exception of that which decorated her crown or sat on her brow (Ashton 2004c: 56–60). The classical symbolism of the snake as a creature associated with doom was established well before the death of Cleopatra, and since the authors who mention it are themselves part of the classical tradition it is not unreasonable to conclude that the asp theory was linked to Greek literature (Baldwin 1964: 181).

8.2 ANCIENT ATTITUDES TO SUICIDE

Rome played a crucial part in the story of Cleopatra's suicide, although it is important to stress that in taking her own life the queen gained some respite from her critics. In ancient Greek culture suicide by poisoning was a means of executing prisoners,

Socrates perhaps being one of the more famous historical figures who were forced to take hemlock. A study on self-killing in the classical world was published in 1990 (van Hoof) and includes both mythical and historical instances. Van Hoof considers the various *causae moriendi* or reasons for suicide and concludes that Cleopatra is best placed under the heading of *pudor* or "no longer being who you used to be" (van Hoof 1990: 107–120, especially 115) and within this cause, shame (110) and a willingness to escape captivity (111) seem likely reasons. There are, however, other possible causes which potentially correspond to Cleopatra's situation: despair (85–94) and grief (99–105) are also plausible reasons for the queen's suicide.

The death of Cleopatra's servants is also considered alongside that of the queen. Van Hoof states that there is no earlier precedent prior to "Hellenism" for servants killing themselves on account of their owner (van Hoof 1990: 18). This is not strictly true; the idea of burying servants with the deceased was already present in Dynasty 1 in Egypt. The royal burials at Abydos suggest that the rulers were buried with their servants. There are few accounts in Egypt of real people being culled and buried alongside their owners/family. From the time of the Second Intermediate Period in Egypt shabti/ushabti figurines took the place of real servants. It seems, therefore, that the suicides of Charmion and Eiras might well have stemmed from the concept of the Egyptian tradition of supporting the deceased in the afterlife, as well as showing devotion to the queen.

The Roman written sources praise Cleopatra's bravery in committing suicide. In Horace Cleopatra is portrayed as a licentious figure, but a brave masculine figure "nor did she, like a woman, quail with fear at the thought of what it is that the dagger does." Twice in the same verse Horace refers to her bravery and in the same section there is the reference to her poisoning by means of snake venom. That she chose suicide over capture was seen in Roman eyes as admirable; at least she had, it seems, done the honorable thing.

In book 2 of Velleius Paterculus' *Histories* Cleopatra is portrayed as another example of Antony's weakness rather than being causal in his demise. Antony redeems himself in chapter 87 by committing suicide and then we are told that Cleopatra ended her life "untouched by a woman's fears" by the poison of an asp. Cleopatra's bravery is alluded to within the context of her death by Josephus (*Jewish War* 1 20.3.396–7) and appears in ode 37 of Horace, who wrote: "she grew fiercer as she beheld her death. Bravely, as if unmoved, she looked upon the ruins of her palace; bravery reached out and touched the poison snakes, and picked them up, and handled them, and held them to her so her heart might drink its fill of their black venom" (trans. Ferry 1997: 97).

Suicide rarely appears in Egyptian literature. Officials were permitted to take their own lives following the Harem conspiracy during the reign of Ramesses III, who ruled from around 1184–1153 BCE (Taylor 2001: 41). The only other well-documented suicide was later than the reign of Cleopatra VII – that of Antinous, the beloved of the Emperor Hadrian, who drowned in the Nile in CE 130 (Lambert 1984: 128–42). This particular suicide or accident – the sources are rife with speculation – is different because those who drowned were believed to be blessed (Taylor 2001: 41). The Emperor Hadrian deified Antinous and a successful cult dedicated to the new god spread from Egypt throughout the Roman world.

There is also a much earlier Middle Kingdom text (Papyrus Berlin 3024; Faulkner 1956: 21–40) in which a man pleads with his soul to end his life. The man states that his name is detested more than the smell of vultures (Faulkner 1956: 27, line 87), and compares death to "a sick man becoming well, like going out of doors after detention" (Faulkner 1956: 29, line 131). However, there is no evidence that I can see from Faulkner's reading of the text to suggest that the man intends to take his own life. He is pleading with his soul to leave his body so that he might go through the necessary rites of passage into the next life. The speaker in the text criticizes his soul for failing to ease the misery he suffers and pleads with the soul to see sense. As Faulkner points out in his commentary on the text, the last two lines recall the scene of the soul returning to the body after death and that according to ancient Egyptian beliefs, if the man died of natural causes and was buried in the correct manner, there was nothing to prevent the soul from returning and allowing him to be reborn in the afterlife (1956: 40).

For Egyptians the key to the afterlife was that their mortal body remained intact to allow the person's spirit to return to the corpse. Once the deceased had managed to answer a series of questions and had shown that their heart (and so conscience) was pure and quite literally lighter than the feather of justice, they would be reborn in the afterlife when the sun shone upon them for one hour of every night (Taylor 2001: 15–44). Thus, the key to an Egyptian was for the body to remain intact. As many modern biographers point out, Cleopatra was not only a queen but also a living goddess and, as such, would not, we are told, fear death. This point of view is somewhat simplified and whilst there are reports of the population celebrating the death, and so re-birth, of a king in the form of Osiris, Cleopatra as Isis does not transform into Hathor of the West quite so easily.

Egyptian rulers were awarded a funerary cult, where the deceased would be tended to by priests. These temples were usually distinct from the tomb, where the body would rest, and represent the symbolic continuation of tending for the spirit of the deceased. This concept is different from the Ptolemaic posthumous cults of the rulers and queens, where in death the person is transformed into a deity. In traditional Egyptian contexts the deceased is celebrated in the state of being dead rather than simply commemorating their life and transition. The cult of Arsinoe II falls somewhere in between the two concepts. Here we see the queen accepted into the pantheon of gods, but only her death has enabled her to be awarded this promotion.

When, therefore, modern historians suggest there was no need for Cleopatra to strive for immortality on account of her status as a living goddess (Whitehorne 1994: 193) they do not fully understand the Egyptian concept of death. This notion is quite separate from that of the living goddess. Cleopatra would continue to be worshipped as a goddess but, in her role as mortal ruler, it was imperative that she should ensure she would pass through the judgment into the next life. Of course here we assume that Cleopatra practised Egyptian religion. If deceased members of the royal family were buried according to Egyptian rites as early as the third century BC, it seems likely that a ruler in the first century would be awarded the same honors. If, after all, the Egyptians were wrong then everything was in place for a Greek afterlife; vice versa would not work.

8.3 MURDER – AN ALTERNATIVE THEORY

There is no ancient conspiracy theory regarding Octavian's part in Cleopatra's death. In the late nineteenth century, however, some modern historians questioned Octavian's degree of involvement (Whitehorne 1994: 194). The question was not so much one of Octavian murdering Cleopatra, but rather of facilitating her suicide by not providing guards to watch over her. As Whitehorne points out, a queen would not have been incarcerated in the same manner as a non-royal prisoner (1994: 195) and he points to the two earlier references to her attempted suicide in Plutarch to indicate that her intent was unquestionable. It is of course possible that Plutarch was setting the scene for the finale of his narrative. Whitehorne is clearly aware of this literary device and refers to it earlier in his chapter on the death of Cleopatra, but he uses the references here to illustrate her determination to die. I note this point to illustrate how easily the historian can accept the parts of a narrative that support his or her arguments and reject those sections that do not.

More recently a television one-hour special made by Atlantic productions for Discovery Channel USA/Channel 5 turned its attentions to the death of the queen. Entitled *The mysterious death of Cleopatra*, a criminal profiler – Pat Brown – used selective Roman sources in order to determine whether Cleopatra committed suicide or whether she was murdered. None of the Roman sources question whether Cleopatra took her own life. In fact several writers, both modern and ancient, seem keen to stress Octavian's compassionate treatment of the deceased Mark Antony and the queen. Whether this apparent compassion concealed a murderer rather than the leader's wish to display Cleopatra in his victory parade will never be known. There is, however, nothing to support this theory. Psychological profiles of deceased rulers from secondary sources are of little help in establishing whether someone was capable of suicide. The ancient accounts are equally problematic but do at least allow us to see the official Roman account of Cleopatra's death.

In 1990 an article was written which concluded that Cleopatra suffered from Narcissistic Personality Disorder (Orland et al. 1990: 169–75). NPD is described as a pervasive pattern of grandiosity, either real or fantasy. People suffering with this condition crave admiration and have a lack of empathy with others. Indicators can be five or more of the following: inflated sense of self worth, sufferers exaggerating their achievements; fantasizing about success, beauty, brilliance, power, or ideal love; believing that they are special or unique; requiring excessive admiration; having unreasonable expectations; taking advantage of others to achieve their aims; being unwilling to identify or recognize the feelings of others; being envious of others or believing others to be envious of them; displaying arrogant attitudes. Cleopatra's critics clearly thought that she suffered from NPD, although obviously they did not have access to such a diagnosis. It is perhaps relevant that most historical leaders, as described in the literary sources, appear to share some of the above characteristics. I cannot help but suggest that the fact Cleopatra was a woman makes personality traits that she displayed, and that are often encouraged in male figures, unacceptable or objectionable.

8.4 EARLIER AND CONTEMPORARY BURIAL PRACTICES

In the third century BCE some Greeks in Alexandria were cremated and their ashes stored in a form of vase more usually used to carry water (a *hydria*). During the early part of the twentieth century many such vases were found in the eastern funerary district of Hadra in Alexandria and as a consequence the vases, which were often inscribed with the name of the deceased, became known as *Hadra hydriai*. Analysis has shown that many examples were imported from the Greek island of Crete and then customized by Alexandrians. It was not long, however, before local Egyptian craftsmen began to copy the form of vase and decoration, thus allowing the family of the deceased to choose a relevant scene to illustrate the occupation or favorite pastime of their relative. It is also possible that such vases were commissioned before death (Lightfoot in Walker and Higgs eds. 2001: 117–20).

Other Alexandrians, presumably the elite, were interred in elaborately decorated tombs. Some of these burial chambers had Egyptian features, but they were predominantly Greek in the style of their decoration and coffins. All of these tombs are rock-cut and so below ground level, reached by stairways (Venit 2002: 46). Those in the Pharos district of Anfushi (tomb 2) show that traditional Egyptian tomb scenes and architectural features in quintessentially Greek tombs were produced as early as the second century BCE (Venit 2002: 77–85). The tombs at Mustafa Pasha/Kamel are similar (Fedak 1990: 131–2). Tomb number 1 at the site consists of Greek-style architecture and paintings but has sphinxes protecting the entrances to the various rooms (Venit 2002: 50–61). The use of sphinxes in the Mustafa Pasha tombs is closer to the Greek tradition, where animals, often lions, guard tombs of the fourth century BCE. In the Egyptian tradition sphinxes usually protect the processional walkways of temples. These tombs would have belonged to a wealthy Greek citizen but are not monumental in the sense that the royal tombs would have been.

There are two further tombs worth considering in this context. The first is the so-called Alabaster tomb (Bonacasa and Minà 2000), which has traditionally been associated with the tomb of Alexander. It has often been assumed that this single stone structure stood above a series of underground chambers. Recent soundings below the structure have disproved this hypothesis (Empereur pers. comm. 2004). The tomb is in an area now called the Latin Cemetery, which is just outside the area identified as the center of the ancient city. Although its form has been compared to Macedonian tombs, the alabaster tomb is more shrine-like in appearance, and may have functioned as part of the chapel for a burial or quite simply as a shrine.

One of the few surviving monumental tombs is in a down-scaled form of the Pharos lighthouse and lies outside Alexandria on Lake Mareotis at Taposiris Magna (Empereur 2002: 222–5). Underneath the structure is a small tomb. The tombs are cut into the bedrock and date to the second century BCE; it is not clear whether the quarter-sized model of the lighthouse originally functioned as a tomb or whether it was simply adopted as a tomb marker (Empereur 2002: 225). Fedak (1990: 133) suggests that the structure was part of the original tomb design.

There was also the mausoleum of Alexander and the Ptolemaic royal family, which was known as the *sema* or *soma*. The Alexandrian mausoleum was Alexander's second tomb; his body was initially placed at the old capital of Memphis (Hölbl 2001: 15), presumably whilst the new capital was being developed. Ancient literary sources indicate that Ptolemy I established a cult to Alexander at his tomb and that the Ptolemaic royal family were buried close to the ruler (Hölbl 2001: 169–70). These sources are corroborated by the eponymous priesthoods that were established to serve the cults of the deceased Ptolemaic rulers and their queens (Ashton 2003a: 123–8 for summary). During the reign of Ptolemy IV (222–204 BCE) the tomb of Alexander was rebuilt (Zenobius 3.94 and Strabo 18.1.8) and reforms were made to the royal cults. The tomb and chapel complex was expanded and the style changed to incorporate a pyramid, thus making the tomb more Egyptian in its form, mimicking the tomb chapels of the New Kingdom.

The cult of Ptolemy I and Berenice I had originally remained separate from that of Alexander, but the cult of Ptolemy II and Arsinoe II had been joined to Alexander's cult. During the Ptolemaia festival of 215/14 BCE Ptolemy IV also moved the cult of the Theoi Soteres (Ptolemy I and his queen) into the main royal cult. The reason for the original separation is not clear; it is possible that the close relationship between Alexander and one of his generals was not seen to be appropriate. As part of Ptolemy IV's reforms a dynastic cult was also initiated in the south at Ptolemais and a new mausoleum (the *sema*) was built in Alexandria. This tomb incorporated not only the cults, but also the bodies of the deceased rulers. The combined tomb was still *in situ* when Octavian visited Alexandria and famously knocked off the nose of Alexander when he embraced the body (Dio LI, 16 and LXXV, 13).

This would imply that the rulers had been buried rather than cremated and there is further evidence, as noted, from the Canopus decree dating to the reign of Ptolemy III, on the mummification of Princess Berenice. This demonstrates that the royal family were buried according to Egyptian rites (Hölbl 2001: 109). Since the cult of Cleopatra VII continued into the late fourth century CE, it seems likely that she too was given full Egyptian burial rites, but no record of this has survived. Some modern historians assume that both Cleopatra and Mark Antony were mummified (Grimm 2003: 48). In contrast cremation was common in Rome in the first century BCE, and so would have been the expected choice for Antony, thus there is little reason to suppose that this was not the case (Walker 1985: 7 on the cremation of Augustus). Cremation seems an unlikely option and there were no parallels for royal cremation in Egypt. The words used by Plutarch for the burial place of Mark Antony and the building in which Cleopatra committed suicide (the Greek words *to taphno* and *to domation* suggest a tomb and mausoleum) (Pelling 1988: 316, 322).

There are earlier Egyptian royal funerary temples and tombs on which Cleopatra may well have modeled her own. The funerary temple of Hatshepsut on the west bank at Thebes offers a possible parallel for Cleopatra's tomb chapel. This imposing building celebrates the achievements of one of Egypt's few female kings in a traditional manner, but is also strong in terms of representing the female relatives of the newly deceased female king. Built close to the site of an earlier temple, dating to the Middle Kingdom, the temple of Hatshepsut is an imposing monument to the deceased ruler. The relief decorations catalogue the ruler's achievements and show her power in fulfilling the role of king.

Another obvious model for the mausoleum of Cleopatra VII could be the aforementioned tomb chapel of the Twenty-fifth-Dynasty royal god's wife, Shepenwpet I, and Amenirdas, also on the West Bank at Thebes, within the earlier "mortuary" temple of Ramesses III at Medinat Habu (Plates 4.1 and 4.2). The chapel scenes show the deified deceased being worshipped by her successor. Like Cleopatra VII these women were divine through their position and enjoyed increased power as a consequence of their divine status as wives of the god Amun (Markoe and Capel 2006: 115–16).

8.5 CLEOPATRA'S MAUSOLEUM

Classicists assume that the form of Cleopatra's mausoleum was Greek. Most "reconstructions" feature a building that is not dissimilar to the fourth-century tombs such as the tomb of Mausolos at Halikarnassos, with an underground chamber and elevated first floor. Pfrommer (Grimm 2003: 48–9) has reconstructed a hypothetical plan of the tomb of Cleopatra; it is wholly Greek in style. The proposed building has a ground and first floor, with decorative columns *in antis* and a door on the ground level. The first floor has windows and the inside shows at least one staircase to this level and a gallery to allow light throughout the building. Whitehorne also questioned the validity of Cleopatra's dedication to Egyptian culture, stating that she was a Macedonian Greek and appeared as such on her coinage (1994: 193). Recent work has shown that Cleopatra was much more Egyptian than Greek and we must not forget that her mausoleum was in many respects a monument of intense personal sentiment, in contrast to the coins which were issued with international and political ends in view.

There is no evidence to support the hypothesis that Cleopatra's tomb was wholly Greek in style. At the very least one might expect some Egyptian symbolism, as found in some of the early tombs of Alexandria, as described above. Plutarch and Dio claim that the building was on two levels. As we have seen, ancient writers use the symbolism of the first floor in order to illustrate the weakness of Mark Antony (whose helpless, injured body was hauled up there), and of Cleopatra, who was effectively trapped with her remaining treasures. Scholars have assumed that the tomb was therefore Greek in style. Some of the Egyptian funerary temples, such as the aforementioned temple of Hatshepsut at Deir el Bahri, are tiered; and Ptolemaic temples have steps within them to a first floor. The Temple of Hathor at Denderah is perhaps the most relevant in terms of its date and association with Cleopatra VII. Much depends on the size of the tomb and its chapel and whether the building, in which Cleopatra is said to have barricaded herself, was quite literally the tomb in which she intended to be interred or whether it was an associated building, perhaps even a treasury.

8.6 LOCATION OF THE TOMB OF CLEOPATRA VII

Cleopatra's mausoleum has not been found, or at least not recognized, by archaeologists. As a consequence, even here we are dependent, as mentioned above, upon the literary sources for descriptions of the building, which, if the sources are accurate, played a crucial role in the queen's final days. Few modern writers consider models for the building and indeed the method of interment fit for the ruler of Egypt. We are dependant once again upon the literary sources for the location of the tomb. Plutarch (*Life of Antony* 74) states that the mausoleum of Cleopatra was close to a (*naos*) shrine/temple of the goddess Isis. We are told that the area was full of high buildings of great beauty. However, no indication of which part of the city is given by any of the ancient authors. Recent fieldwork in Alexandria may help to establish where Cleopatra's temple of Isis was located, and this in turn may lead us to the district in which the mausoleum was housed. The tomb of Cleopatra is thought to have been independent of the tomb of Alexander and the Ptolemies. It is also thought to have been unfinished at the time of the literary accounts of her suicide, as reported in Plutarch and Dio. Once again we are dependent upon the Roman literary sources for this information, but it was normal practice both within Egyptian and Roman cultural contexts for a ruler to build their own tomb during their lifetime.

In 2003 it was suggested that the mausoleum of Cleopatra VII may be associated with the temple of Isis in the eastern quarter of Alexandria, known today as Smouha and on the borders of ancient Hadra and Eleusis (Ashton 2003a: 120–2). The aforementioned sanctuary's appearance can be pieced together from descriptions of the site by eighteenth-century travelers and from the finds that can be associated with the site. These include a colossal dyad (chapter 6 above), columns, sphinxes, a *tholos* (round temple), and a granite elephant (Ashton forthcoming 2007b). The latter has parallels in the Roman period and suggests that the site continued to be occupied during the Roman occupation. However, until further exploration of the site, now beneath a number of schools, a bus park, a police station, and private land (Ashton 2005b), the suggestion that the mausoleum was positioned here, in the eastern quarter of the city, must remain speculative. The Isis sanctuary accords with the mention of this temple with regard to the tomb in Plutarch (*Life of Antony* 74).

Passengers on Egypt Air in January and February 2006 were able to read about another suggested resting place for Cleopatra in Taposiris Magna, which is close to Alexandria on Lake Mareotis. Work has begun there, following a suggestion by a Classical archaeologist from the University of the Dominican Republic (K. Martinez) that the tomb of Cleopatra may be in this vicinity. According to the article, excavations will be under the direction of the Egyptian Supreme Council of Antiquities (Hawass 2006: 22). And so the search for Cleopatra continues.

9

THE LEGACY OF CLEOPATRA

9.1 THE ROMAN VICTORY

The victory of Octavian in autumn of 29 BCE as recorded in Dio Cassius (book 51, chapters 21–2):

> The other possessions were remarkable . . . , but the most extravagant and stunning was that commemorating Egypt. Among other items was carried a statue of Cleopatra lying in a representation of her death on a couch, so that in a way she too could be seen in procession with the other prisoners and with her children, Alexander Helios and Cleopatra Selene. After he had finished these celebrations, Octavian dedicated the temple of Minerva (also known as the Chalcidicum), and the Curia Iulia, built in honour of his father. In this he sent up the statue of Victory, which is still there, claiming, so it seems, that it was from her that he received the Empire. The statue had belonged to the people of Tarentum, and was brought from here to Rome, set up in the Senate House and decorated with the spoils of Egypt. (trans. Meadows 2001: 14)

Coins with crocodiles representing Egypt were minted to celebrate Octavian's victory. In Gaul a version even showed the crocodile tethered to a palm tree and with a victory wreath. In this way, outside Egypt the Roman victory was celebrated.

9.2 EGYPT IN AUGUSTAN ROME

In 27 BCE Octavian was awarded the title Augustus by the Roman Senate, and the ruler declared himself the first citizen of the newly restored Republic, the first emperor of Rome. Although the emperor was openly hostile towards Egyptian culture and religion, he nevertheless used Egyptian imagery to promote his victory over Cleopatra. The temples dedicated by Augustus in Egypt were a blatant means of promoting his new position as the country's ruler. When asked if he wanted to see the Apis bull at Memphis, however, he declined (Dio 51.16). Obelisks were brought from Egypt to Rome and were placed in the Campus Martius and the Circus Maximus (Alfano 2001: 286). Furthermore there were many Egyptian elements that were incorporated into the design of Augustus' own mausoleum. This mausoleum was started soon after the emperor's return to Rome and, it has been suggested, was used as a direct political parallel to Mark Antony who had stipulated in his will that he wished to be buried in Egypt with Cleopatra (Zanker 1990: 72–7). The Egyptian obelisks at the entrance of this sizeable tomb were placed at the front as a reference to Augustus' victory over his rival. Strabo (*Geography* 5.3.9) described the structure, its statue of Augustus, and the gardens that lay behind it. The building was later to be decorated with the *Res Gestae* – a catalogue of Augustus' achievements during his long reign.

It was not really until later in the first century CE that "Egyptomania" took hold in Rome. It was during the reign of the Emperor Domitian, in particular, that the Imperial house actively promoted Egyptian cults. This present book is not the place to discuss these initiatives in any real detail. Egypt's popularity during the first and second centuries CE was, however, doubtless largely a result of Cleopatra, not only in the sense that her defeat heralded Roman control of the province, but because, like the Ptolemies before them, many of the Roman emperors enjoyed the exotic nature of its culture.

It is necessary to make a distinction between Egyptian cults and temples, and themed decorative schemes such as those from

Herculaneum and Pompeii in the mid-first century CE. The *Aula Isiaca* on the Palatine Hill in Rome offers a good example of the latter category of Egyptian decorative schemes and is most probably closer in date to the reign of Augustus, most likely dating to the reign of Caligula who was himself descended from Mark Antony's line. Amongst the images are cobras, *situlae* (rattles), and lotus flowers, clearly intended as a reference to Egypt and/or Egyptian cults (Iacopi 1997).

Recently, a new interpretation of the decorative relief on a cameo glass vase, often called the "Portland Vase," has linked the glass vessel to Cleopatra and Mark Antony (Walker 2004). The vase was made during the reign of Augustus. There have been a number of suggested interpretations of the vase's decorative scheme (Walker 2004: 41–63). The overall priciple is concerned with the seduction of the key male figure by a reclining female, which, as Walker has recently proposed, has an obvious link to the story of Antony and Cleopatra, particularly with regard to its telling by Roman writers. In the newly proposed reading Cleopatra and Mark Antony, accompanied by Eros, appear on one side of the vase; on the other Octavia lies on the remains of a fallen structure and is flanked by Octavian to the viewer's left and Venus, a reference to Venus Genetrix, patron of their family, to the right. Other examples of cameo glass may also refer to the story of Antony and Cleopatra and the subsequent victory of Augustus for Rome (Walker 2004: 61–3).

9.3 CLEOPATRA AND MARK ANTONY: POSTHUMOUS PRESENTATIONS

It would be wrong to presume that fascination with Cleopatra and the development of her "myth" are modern concepts. As seen by the level of discussion surrounding her death (Plutarch, Dio), the last queen of Egypt was a figure who attracted great interest and intrigue during her lifetime and in the period immediately after. It is of little surprise, therefore, that Cleopatra was posthumously represented. Mark Antony's line of course continued through the Roman emperor Claudius who was descended from Antony and Octavia.

During the first century CE a number of Nilotic motifs were incorporated into the decorative schemes of both houses and sanctuaries in Italy. Some have been directly linked to Cleopatra. Two examples found in Pompeii and Herculaneum in southern Italy reveal images in the form of a profile view of a royal female that is similar to the portrait on the coins of Cleopatra (Walker and Higgs 2001: 314–15, no. 325). The example from Herculaneum is perhaps the closer of the two and clearly shows the *nodus* (knot) of hair and broad diadem; the prominent earring is also a feature of some of the coin images. The face is youthful with a strong straight nose, full lips, and an angular chin. The neck is decorated with the usual "Venus" rings that were so common on the portraits of Ptolemaic queens.

In addition to this form of representation there are a number of more comic caricatures that have been identified as Cleopatra and Mark Antony. They form part of a series of decorative reliefs or paintings that show Nilotic scenes, often, but not always, of a debauched nature. It has been suggested that such images were one way in which the Romans promoted their victory at the battle of Actium and attempted to discredit Cleopatra (Walker 2003c: 202). One particular example that seems to refer directly to the fallen couple is now housed in the British Museum and was included in the 2001 Cleopatra of Egypt exhibition (Walker and Higgs 2001: 336, no. 356; Walker 2003b: 191–2). Amidst a Nilotic landscape a pygmy wearing a marsh-dweller's cap steers a boat with a canopy. Beneath this canopy is a couple engaged in sexual intercourse – the hair style suggests that the woman, who is penetrated from the rear, is Cleopatra and that her partner of course is Mark Antony. The relief has been dated from the first century BCE to the first century CE. The Nilotic paintings and terracotta reliefs of a more general nature are widely accepted to date to the the reigns of the later Julio-Claudian emperors – Caligula, Claudius, and Nero – and so from around 37–68 CE (Walker 2003c: 200–1). As noted previously these rulers were descended from Mark Antony and Octavia, and it has been suggested that there may well have been an increase in Roman interests of things Egyptian in this period.

Although at first sight many of these images seem, to modern eyes, contemptuous, it is necessary to view them within an ancient context, and also to consider the cultural context. A lamp, for instance, has long been cited as an example of a caricature of the queen (Walker and Higgs 2001: 337, no. 357). The top surface of the lamp is decorated with an image of a female pygmy standing on a crocodile signifying Egypt, holding a palm branch in her right hand and sitting on a phallus. The figure has been identified as Cleopatra on account of the styling of her hair, which is drawn back in the familiar bun. It has more recently been suggested that this lamp may have been part of the Isis cult and that the phallus was a direct reference to that of the Egyptian god Osiris (Etienne 2003). According to this myth, Isis collected the scattered body parts of her brother and husband Osiris and impregnated herself by using the phallus. Although the lamp is Roman in terms of its material culture, Roman initiates to the the Isis cult would have been aware of the Osiris myth and no doubt Cleopatra's link to the goddess. When considered in this light the scene becomes a more respectful reference to Cleopatra, a number of years after her death.

9.5 ISIS

The links between Cleopatra and Isis during the Roman period were not, however, limited to caricatures on lamps and decorative schemes. It is difficult to know if Isis initiates were aware that the type of image adopted to represent the goddess during the Roman period was originally that used for statues of defied Ptolemaic queens, as discussed earlier in chapter 6. Many of the components of these portrayals found their way onto the presentation of Isis during the first century CE in both Egypt and Rome. It has been suggested that the adoption of features such as the cornucopia (horn of plenty), knotted costume, and locks of hair – all of which became synonymous with Isis in the Roman world – were taken from the Ptolemaic queen iconographic repertoire

(Ashton 2003c: 34; 2004c: 49). In a small way the adoption statues that originally represented Ptolemaic queens by those engaged in Isis cults meant that Cleopatra VII continued to be honored as a goddess; she had after all believed herself to be a new version of the queen. With this in mind the aforementioned references in the form of reliefs, paintings, lamps, and vases seem to make considerably more sense. Cleopatra may not have been liked by the Roman writers, but she remained a subject of speculation, gossip, and legend, and she continues to do so today.

9.6 THE FATE OF CLEOPATRA'S CHILDREN

This final chapter seems a fitting place in which to consider the fate of Cleopatra's four children. Plutarch (*Life of Antony* 81) states that Ptolemy Caesar, who was "supposed to be Cleopatra's son by Julius Caesar," was sent to India via Ethiopia, but was tricked into returning by the promise that Octavian would make him king of Egypt. He would have been between 13 and 15 years old. Octavian was said to have said "it is bad to have too many Caesars," parodying *Illiad* book 2.204. Ptolemy Caesar was of course put to death (chapter 82). Suetonius (*Deified Augustus*) records that the three remaining children survived.

The remaining three children (the twins who were ten and Philadelphos who was six) were in fact brought to Rome and were raised in the house of Antony's official widow, Octavia. Suetonius notes that Octavian treated the children as if they were his own family (*Deified Augustus* 48). We hear nothing more of the two boys – Alexander Helios and Ptolemy Philadelphos – but Cleopatra Selene survived and became the wife of Juba, a client king, who ruled Mauretania, now modern Algeria (Roller 2003: 91–118).

The artistic and cultural programmes of Cleopatra Selene and Juba were heavily influenced by their own native backgrounds (Roller 2003: 119). The two main cities of Mauretania were Volubilis and Iol (also Caesarea/Cherchel); it was at Iol where the new capital was established.

There is a portrait from the site made according to a classical style that may well represent Cleopatra VII (Walker and Higgs 2001: 219, no. 197). It shows an older version of the aforementioned Vatican and Berlin heads that were manufactured in Rome, and quite possibly may have been produced during Cleopatra VII's lifetime and perhaps taken as a momento by her daughter. The usual snail-shell curls and strong profile are present, but it is not known if these features were exclusive to Cleopatra VII or if they were copied by her daughter. It has subsequently been suggested that this marble head may represent Cleopatra Selene rather than Cleopatra VII (Ferroukhi 2003).

Egyptian statues have also been found at the site (Roller 2003: 142–4), including a representation of Petubastes the high priest of Memphis, who died on July 31, 30 BCE, aged 16 (Roller 2003: fig. 17). One day later Octavian took control of Alexandria. Cleopatra Selene may have taken the statue to remind her of this difficult time and perhaps the fact that she survived in spite of her parents' deaths or, more likely, that the young Memphite priest was a friend or someone known to the girl. She was ten years old at this time.

Other Egyptian sculptures date to earlier periods of Egyptian history (Roller 2003: 142–4) and include a statue of the Eighteenth-Dynasty ruler Thutmose I, a uraeus, and a head of Ammon. Other material from the site is Egyptianizing and dates to the Roman period, showing that a strong connection was maintained with the last descendent of the Ptolemaic royal family – Ptolemy, son of Cleopatra Selene and Juba.

The demise of this final Ptolemy, Cleopatra VII's only known grandchild, is highly ironic, although perhaps of little surprise. He was not the only descendent of Mark Antony – as noted the Emperor Gaius (better known as Caligula) continued the line of Octavia and Antony. Caligula clearly saw his cousin as a political threat but it is said that he ordered his execution on account of his envy of Ptolemy's dress, according to some sources in the form of a purple cloak (Roller 2003: 254). With his death the Ptolemaic royal line came to an end.

BIBLIOGRAPHY

Abd al-Galil, O. 2000. *Tarikh Misr li-Yohana Al-Niqusi*. Cairo.

Albersmeier, S., 2002. *Untersuchungen zu den Frauenstatuen des Ptolemäischen Ägypten*. Mainz am Rhein: Verlag Philipp Von Zabern.

Alfano, C., 2001. "Egyptian influences in Italy," in Walker and Higgs eds., 276–89.

Amer, H. I., and Morardet, B., 1983. "Les dates de la construction du temple majeur d'Hathor à Dendara à l'époque gréco-romaine," *Annals du Service des Antiquités de L'Egypte* 69: 255–8.

Andreae, B. et al., eds. 2006. *Kleopatra und die Caesaren*. Munich: Hirmer Verlag.

Arnold, Dieter, 1999. *Temples of the last pharaohs*. New York: Oxford University Press.

Arnold, Dorothea., ed. 1996. *Royal women of Amarna*. New York: Metropolitan Muesum of Art.

Arnold, Dorothea, 1996. "An artistic revolution: the early years of King Amenhotep IV/Akhenaten," in Arnold ed., 17–39.

—— 2005. "The temple of Hatshepsut at Deir el Bahri," in Roehrig ed., 135–40.

Ashton, S-A., 2000. "The Ptolemaic royal influence on Egyptian royal sculpture," in Riggs and McDonald eds., 1–10.

—— 2001a. *Ptolemaic royal sculpture from Egypt. The interaction between Greek and Egyptian traditions*. British Archaeological Reports International Series 923. Oxford: Archaeopress.

—— 2001b. "Identifying the Egyptian-style Ptolemaic queens," in Walker and Higgs eds., 148–55.

—— 2002a. "A question of authenticity of date? Roman copies and Ptolemaic originals," in *British Museum Studies in Ancient Egypt and Sudan 2*. http://www.thebritishmuseum.ac.uk/research/publications/bmsaes/issue_2.aspx.

—— 2002b. www.britishmuseum.org/research/publications/bmsaes/issue_ldpx.
—— 2003a. *The last queens of Egypt*. Britain: Pearson Education.
—— 2003b. "The Ptolemaic royal image and the Egyptian tradition," in Tait ed., 213–24.
—— 2003c. *Petrie's Ptolemaic and Roman Memphis*. London: Institute of Archaeology.
—— 2003d. "Cleopatra: goddess, ruler or regent?" in Walker and Ashton eds., 25–30.
—— 2004a "Ptolemaic Alexandria and the Egyptian tradition," in Hirst and Silk eds., 15–40.
—— 2004b. "Review of P. E. Stanwick's *Ptolemaic royal portraiture. Greek kings and Egyptian pharaohs*," *Journal of Roman Archaeology* 17: 543–50.
—— 2004c. *Roman Egyptomania*. Great Britain: Golden House Publications.
—— 2005a. "The double and triple uraeus and Egyptian royal women," in Cooke and Simpson eds., 1–10.
—— 2005b. "In search of Cleopatra's temple," *Egyptian Archaeology* 27 (2005): 30–2.
—— Forthcoming 2007a. "Roman uses of Ptolemaic sculpture in Italy," in *Papers in honour of Professor G. B. Waywell*, edited by F. McFarlane and C. Morgan. London: Institute of Classical Studies.
—— Forthcoming 2007b. "In search of the Thesmophorion," in *City and harbour conference*, edited by D. Robinson. Oxford: Centre for Maritime Archaeology Conference.
—— Et al forthcoming. "Report on the 2004 and 2007 fieldwork in Hadra, Alexandria," to be submitted to the *Journal of Egyptian Archaeology* (2008).
Ashton, S-A., and Spanel, D., 2000. "Portraiture," in *Oxford Encyclopaedia of Ancient Egypt*, edited by Donald B Redford. New York: Oxford University Press.
Baldwin, B., 1964. "The death of Cleopatra VII," *Journal of Egyptian Archaeology* 50: 181–2.
Bernal, M., 1991. *Black Athena: The Afroasiatic roots of classical civilisation vol. 1: the fabrication of Classical Greece*. London: Free Association Books/New Brunswick: Rutgers University Press.
—— 2001. *Black Athena: The Afro-asiatic roots of classical civilisation vol. 2: the archaeological and documentary evidence*. London: Free Association Books/New Brunswick: Rutgers University Press.

Bianchi, R. S., 1980. "Not the Isis knot in," *Bulletin of the Egyptological Seminar* 2 (1980): 2, 9–32.
—— ed. 1988. *Cleopatra's Egypt: age of the Ptolemies*. New York: The Brooklyn Museum.
—— 2003. "Images of Cleopatra reconsidered," in Walker and Ashton eds., 13–24.
Bingen, J., 1995. "Les ordonnances royals C. Ord. Ptol. 75–6 (Héracléopolis, 41 avant J.-C)," *Chronique d' Égypte* 70: 206–22.
—— 2007. *Hellenistic Egypt. Monarchy, society, economy, culture*. Edinburgh: Edinburgh University Press.
Bird, H. W., 1994. Liber de Caesaribus *of Sectus Aurelius Victor*. Liverpool: Liverpool University Press.
Bonacasa, N., and Minà, P., eds. 2000. *Achille Adriani: la tomba di Alessandro, realtà, ipotesi e fantasie. Documenti e ricerche d'arte alessandrina* 6. Rome: L'Erma di Bretschneider.
Botti, G. 1892 *Il museo di Alessandria e gli scavi nell'anno 1892*. Alexandria.
Bradford, E., 1971. *Cleopatra*. Harmondsworth: Penguin Books (repr. 2000).
Bulloch, A., Gruen, E. S., Long, A. A., and Stewart, A., eds. 1993. *Images and ideologies: self-definition in the Hellenistic world*. Papers presented at a conference held April 7–9 1998 at the University of California at Berkeley. Berkeley: University of California.
Carcopino, J., 1937. *César et Cléopâtre, Annales de l'école des hautes etudes de Grand*, Vol. 1.
Cauville, S., 1998. *Dendara 1*, Orientalia Lovaniensia Analecta 81. Leuven: Uitgeverij Peeters.
—— 1999. *Dendara 2*, Orientalia Lovaniensia Analecta 88. Leuven: Uitgeverij Peeters.
—— 2000a. *Dendara 3*, Orientalia Lovaniensia Analecta 95. Leuven: Uitgeverij Peeters.
—— 2000b. *Le temple de Dendara 11*, parts 1 and 2, Orientalia Lovaniensia Analecta. Leuven: Uitgeverij Peeters.
—— 2001. *Dendara 4*, Orientalia Lovaniensia Analecta 101. Leuven: Uitgeverij Peeters.
—— 2004a. *Dendara 5–6, Les crypts du temple d'Hathor*, Vol. 1, Orientalia Lovaniensia Analecta 131. Leuven: Uitgeverij Peeters.
—— 2004b. *Dendara, Les crypts du temple d'Hathor*, Vol. 2, Orientalia Lovaniensia Analecta 132. Leuven: Uitgeverij Peeters.

Charles, R. H., 1916. *The* Chronicle *of John Bishop of Nikiu*. London, Oxford: Published for the Text and Translation Society by Williams & Norgate.

Chauveau, M. 2000. *Egypt in the age of Cleopatra*. Ithaca and London: Cornell Press.

—— 2002. *Cleopatra beyond the myth*. Ithaca and London: Cornell Press.

Clarke, J. H., 1984. "African warrior queens," in van Sertima ed., 126–7.

Clarysse, W., forthcoming 2007. "Two Ptolemaic stelae from the sacred lion of Leonton Polis (Tell Moqdam)," *Chronique D'Égypte*.

Clarysse, W., Schoors, A., and Willems, H., eds. 1998–9. *Egyptian religion, the last thousand years. Studies dedicated to the memory of Jan Quaegebeur*. 2 vols. Louvain: Orientalia Lovaniensia Analecta 84 & 85.

Cooke, A., and Simpson, F., eds. 2005. *Current research in Egyptology* 2. BAR International Series 1380. Oxford: Archaeopress.

El Daly, O., 2004. *Egyptology, the missing millennium: Ancient Egypt in medieval arab writings*. Routledge: London.

Delia, D., 1993. "Response to Samuel," in Green ed., 192–203.

Devauchelle, D., 1985. "De nouveau la construction du temple d' Hathor à Dendara," *Review d'Egyptologie* 36: 172–4.

Devauchelle, D., 2001. "La stèle du Louvre IM 8 (Sérapéum de Memphis) et la prétendue date de naissance de Césarion," *Enchoria* 27 (2001): 41–61.

Dils, P., 1998. "La couronne d'Arsinoe Philadelphe," in Clarysse et al. eds., Vol. 2, 1309–30.

Dorman, P., 2005. "Hatshepsut: princess to queen to co-ruler," in Roehrig ed., 87–90.

Dunand, F., 1998. "Priest bearing an Osiris-Canopus in his veiled hands," in Goddio et al. eds., 189–94.

Edwards, C. 2000. *Suetonius. Lives of the Caesars*. Oxford: Oxford University Press.

Empereur, J-Y., 2002. *Alexandria rediscovered*. London: British Museum Press.

Etienne, M., 2003. "Queen, harlot of lecherous goddess?" in Walker and Ashton eds., 95–102.

Faulkner, R. O., 1956. "The man who was tired of life," *Journal of Egyptian Archaeology* 42 (1956): 21–40.

Fedak, J., 1990. *Monumental tombs of the Hellenistic age*. Canada: University of Toronto Press.

Ferroukhi, M., 2003. "Les Deux Portraits de Chercehll Présumés Cleopâtre VII," in Walker and Ashton eds., 103–8.

Ferry, D., 1997. *Odes of Horace*. New York: Farrar, Straus and Giroux.

Foss, M., 1997. *In search of Cleopatra*. Great Britain: Michael O'Mara Books.

Fraser, P. M., 1972. *Ptolemaic Alexandria*. Oxford: Oxford University Press (repr. 1998).

Garuti, I., 1958. *Carmen de Bello Actiaco*. Bellum Actiacum: e Papyro Herculanensi 817. Bologna: N. Zanichelli.

Gauthier, H., 1916. *Le livre des rois d'Égypte: recueil de titres et protocols royaux, noms propres de rois, reines, princes, princesses et parents de rois 4: De la XXVe Dynastie à la fin des Ptolémées*. MIFAO 20. Cairo: Institut Français d'Archéologie Orientale.

Goddio, F., Bernand, A., Bernand, E., and Darwish, I., eds. 1998. *Alexandria. The submerged royal quarters*. London: Periplus.

Goddio, F., and Claus, M., eds. 2006. *Egypt's sunken treasures*. Berlin: Prestel.

Gowing, A. M., 1992. *The triumphal narratives of Appion and Cassius Dio*. Ann Arbor: University of Michigan Press.

Grajetzki, W., 2005. *Ancient Egyptian queens: a hieroglyphic dictionary*. London: Golden House Publications.

Grant, M. 1972. *Cleopatra*. St. Albans: Panther Books.

Green, P., ed. 1993. *Hellenistic history and culture*. Berkeley: University of California Press.

Griffiths, J. G., 1961. "The death of Cleopatra VII," *Journal of Egyptian Archaeology* 47 (1961): 113–18.

Grimm, G., 2003. "Alexandria at the time of Cleopatra," in Ashton and Walker eds., 45–50.

Gruen, E., 2003. "Cleopatra in Rome: facts and fantasies," in *Myth, History and Culture in Republican Rome*, edited by D. Braund and C. Gill. Exeter: University of Exeter Press, 257–74.

Haase, W., and Temporini, H., eds. 1995. *Aufsteig und Niedergang der römischen Welt*. Berlin: De Gruyter.

Habachi, L., 1987 (repr.). *Obelisks*. Cairo: American University in Cairo Press.

Haley, S. P., 1993. "Black feminist thought and classics: re-membering, re-claiming, re-empowering," in Rabinowitz and Richlin eds., 23–43.

Hamer, M., 1993. *Signs of Cleopatra: history, politics, representation*. London: Routledge.

—— 2003. "Disowning Cleopatra," in Walker and Ashton eds., 119–26.

Hawass, Z., 2006. "Cleopatra, queen of magic," *Horus magazine*, 20–2.

Hayes, William C., 1957. "Varia from the time of Hatshepsut," *Mitteilungen des Deutschen Archäologischen Instituts, Abteilung Kairo* 15: 78–90.

Hazzard, R. A., 2000. *Imagination of a monarchy: studies in Ptolemaic propaganda*. Toronto: University of Toronto Press.

Heinen, H., 1995. "Vorstufen und Anfänge des Herrscherkultes im Römischen Ägypten," in Haase and Temporini eds., 3144–180.

Herrmann, J., 1988. "Roman Bronzes," in Kozloff and Mitten eds., 288–93.

Higgs, P., 2001. "Searching for Cleopatra's image: Classical portraits in stone," in Walker and Higgs eds., 200–9.

Hirst, A., and Silk, M., eds. 2004. *Alexandria. Real and imagined*. Centre for Hellenic Studies King's College London publication 5. London: Ashgate.

Hölbl, G., 2001. *History of the Ptolemaic Empire*. London: Routledge.

Hughes-Hallet, L., 1990. *Cleopatra: histories, dreams and distortions*. New York: Harper and Row.

Huß, W., 1990. "Die Herkunft der Kleopatra Philopator," *Aegyptus* 70:1–2, Gennaio–Dicembre, 191–204.

Iacopi, I., 1997. *Aula Isiaca Electa*. Milan.

Johansen, F., 2003. "Portraits of Cleopatra, do they exist? An evaluation of the marble heads shown at the British Museum exhibition Cleopatra of Egypt. From History to Myth," in Walker and Ashton eds., 75–80.

Jones, P. J., 2006. *Cleopatra, a source book*. Oklahoma: University of Oklahoma Press.

Joyce, J. W., 1993. *Lucan, Pharsalia*. Ithaca and London: Cornell University Press.

Kiss, Z., 1984. *Etudes sur le portrait imperial roman en Egypte. Travaux du Centre d'archéologie méditerranéenne de l'Académie polonaise des sciences* 23. Warsaw: Editions scientifiques de Pologne.

—— 1998. "The sculptures," in Goddio et al. eds., 169–88.

Kleiner, D. E. E., 2005. *Cleopatra and Rome*. Cambridge, MA and London: Belknap Press of Harvard University Press.

Koenen, L., 1993. "The Ptolemaic king as a religious figure," in Bulloch et al. eds., 25–115.

Kozloff, M. P., and Mitten, D. G. eds. 1988 *The God's delight the human figure in classical bronze*. Cleveland: Cleveland Museum of Art.

Kreuzer, M., 2000. *The coinage system of Cleopatra VII and Augustus in Cyprus*. Springfield MA: Matthew Kreuzer.

Kyrieleis, H., 1975. *Bildnisse der Ptolemäer Archäologische Forschungen* 2. Berlin: Mann.

Lacey, W. K., ed. 1986. *Cicero, Second Philippic Oration*. Warminster, England: Aris & Phillips Publishers.

Lambert, R., 1984. *Beloved and God. The story of Hadrian and Antinous*. London: Phoenix (repr. 1997).

Lefkowitz, M. R., 1996. "Ancient history modern myths," in Lefkowitz and MacLean Rogers eds., 3–26.

Lefkowitz, M. R., and MacLean Rogers, G., eds. 1996. *Black Athena revisited*. Chapel Hill: University of North Carolina Press.

Lepsius, C. R., 1842. *Denkmäler aus Aegypten und Aethiopien: nach den Zeichnungen der von seiner Majestät dem Könige von Preussen Friedrich Wilhelm IV. nach diesen Ländern gesendeten und in den Jahren 1842–1845 ausgeführten wissenschaftlichen Expedition auf Befehl seiner Majestät* 4 . Berlin.

Lightfoot, C., 2001. "*Hadra hydriai*," in Walker and Higgs eds., 117–20.

Maehler, H., 1983. "Egypt under the last Ptolemies," *Bulletin of the Institute of Classical Studies* 30: 1–16.

—— 2003. "Ptolemaic queens with a triple uraeus," *Chronique d'Egypte* 78: 294–303.

Markoe, A. K., and Capel, G. E., eds. 2006. *Mistress of the house, mistress of heaven. Women in ancient Egypt*. New York: Hudson Hills Press in association with Cincinnati Art Gallery.

Marsh, J. ed. 2006. *The black Victorians: Black people in British art 1800–1900*. Aldershot: Lund Press.

Masters, J., 1992. *Poetry and civil war in Lucan's* Bellum Civile. Cambridge: Cambridge University Press.

Meadows, A., 2001. "Sins of the fathers: the inheritance of Cleopatra, last queen of Egypt," in Walker and Higgs eds., 1–14.

Meyboom, P. G. P., 1995. *The Nile mosaic of Palestrina. Early evidence of Egyptian religion in Italy*. Leiden and New York: E.J. Brill.

Mond, R., and Myers, O. H., 1934. *The Bucheum* 2, edited by H. W. Fairman. London: Egypt Exploration Society.

Moreno, P., 1994. *Scultura ellenistica*. Rome: Istituto poligrafico e Zecca dello Stato, Libreria dello Stato.

Muszynski, M., 1977. "Les Associations religieuses en Egypte d'aprés les sources hiéroglyphiques, démotiques et grecques," *Orientalia Lovaniensia Periodica* 8: 145–74.

O'Connor, D., and Reid, A., eds. 2003. *Ancient Egypt in Africa.* Encounters with Ancient Egypt. London: Taylor and Francis.

O'Connor, D., and Reid, A., 2003. "Introduction – locating ancient Egypt in Africa: modern theories, past realities," in O'Connor and Reid eds., 1–22.

Orland, R. et al., 1990. "Psychiatric assessment of Cleopatra: a challenging evaluation," *Psychopathology* 23: 169–75.

Palter, R., 1996. "Black Athena, Afrocentrism, and the history of science," in Lefkowitz, M. R. and MacLean Rogers, G. eds., 209–68.

Patch, D. Craig, 2005. "The shrines to Hathor at Deir el Bahri," in Roehrig ed., 173–5.

Pelling, C. B. R., ed. 1988. *Plutarch. Life of Antony.* Cambridge: Cambridge University Press.

Pomeroy, S. B., 1990 (repr.). *Women in Hellenistic Egypt. From Alexander to Cleopatra.* Detroit: Wayne State University Press.

Quaegebeur, J., 1988. "Cleopatra VII and the cults of the Ptolemaic queens," in Bianchi ed., 41–54.

Rabinowitz, N. S., 1993. "Introduction," in Rabinowitz and Richlin eds., 1–22.

Rabinowitz, N. S., and Richlin, A., 1993. *Feminist theory and the Classics.* New York and London: Routledge.

Ray, J., 2001. "Alexandria," in Walker and Higgs eds., 32–7.

—— 2003. "Cleopatra in the temples of Upper Egypt: the evidence of Dendera and Armant," in Walker and Ashton eds., 9–12.

Riggs, C., and McDonald, A., 2000. *Current research in Egyptology* 1. BAR International Series 909. Oxford: Archaeopress.

Rigsby, K. J. 1996. *Asylia. Territorial inviolability in the Hellenistic world.* Hellenistic Culture and Society. Berkeley: University of California Press.

Robins, G., 1996. *Women in ancient Egypt.* London: British Museum Press.

Roehrig, C., ed. 2005. *Hatshepsut. From queen to pharaoh.* New Haven and London: Yale University Press.

Roller, D., 2003. *The world of Juba II and Kleopatra Selene. Royal scholarship on Rome's African frontier.* New York and London: Routledge.

Roth, A. M., 2005. "Hatshepsut's mortuary temple at Deir el Bahri: architecture as political statement," in Roehrig ed., 147–57.

Rowlandson, J., ed. 1998. *Women and society in Greek and Roman Egypt. A source book.* Cambridge: Cambridge University Press.

Royster, F. T., 2003. *Becoming Cleopatra. The shifting image of an icon.* New York: Palgrave Macmillan.

Russman, E., 1974. *Representation of the king in the 25th Dynasty.* Monographies reine Elisabeth 3. Bruxelles: Fondation egyptologique reine Elisabeth/Brooklyn: Brooklyn Museum.

Samuel, A. E., 1993. "The Ptolemaic ruler as a religious figure," in Green, P. ed., 168–91.

Scott-Kilvert, I., 1965. *Plutarch. Makers of Rome.* London: Penguin Books.

Shackelton Bailey, D. R., ed. 1965–70. *Cicero, Epistolae ad Atticum.* Cambridge: Cambridge University Press.

Shohat, E., 2003. "Disorientating Cleopatra: a modern trope of identity," in Walker and Ashton eds., 127–38.

Slavitt, D. R., 2002. *Propertius in love: the elegies.* Berkeley: University of California Press.

Smith, R. R. R., 1988. *Hellenistic royal portraits.* Oxford: Oxford University Press.

Snowden, F. M., 1996. "Bernal's' 'Blacks' and Afrocentrics," in Lefkowitz and MacLean Rogers eds., 112–28.

Spaer, A., 1999. "The royal male head and Cleopatra at Ascalon," in *Travaux de numismatique grecque offerts à Georges Le Rider,* edited by M. Amandry and S. Hurter. London: Spink, 347–50.

Speigelberg, W., 1925. "Weshalb wählte Kleopatra den Tod durch Schlangenbiss?" in *Ägyptologische Mitteilungen,* Sitzungsb. Munich.

Stanwick, P. E., 2002. *Portraits of the Ptolemies. Greek kings as Egyptian pharaohs.* Austin: University of Texas Press.

Stewart, A. F., 1993. Faces of Power: *Alexander's Image and Hellenistic Politics.* Berkeley: University of California Press.

Tait, W. J., 2003a. *Never had the like occurred: Egypt's view of its past.* Encounters with Ancient Egypt. London: University College London.

Tait, W. J., 2003b. "Cleopatra by name," in Walker and Ashton eds., 3–8.

Taylor, J., 2001. *Death and the afterlife in ancient Egypt.* London: British Museum Press.

Thiers, C., and Volokline, Y., 2005. *Ermant 1. Les crypts du temple ptolémaïque*. Cairo: IFAO.

Thompson, D., 1988. *Memphis under the Ptolemies*. Oxford and Princeton: Princeton University Press.

—— 2000. "Athenaeus in his Egyptian context," in *Athenaeus and his World*, edited by D. Braund and J. Wilkins. Exeter: Exeter University Press, 77–84.

—— 2003. "Cleopatra VII: The queen in Egypt," in Walker and Ashton eds., 31–4.

Townsend, G., 1988. *Caesar's war in Alexandria. Bellum Civile 3*. Bristol: Bristol Classical Press.

Traunecker, C., 1992. *Coptos, Hommes et Dieux sur le parvis de Geb*. Orientalia Lovaniensa Analecta 43. Leuven: Peeters.

Troy, T., 1986. *Patterns of queenship in ancient Egyptian myth and history*. Uppsala Studies in Ancient Mediterranean and Near Eastern Civilisations 14. Uppsala and Stockholm: Almquist & Wiksell.

van Binsbergan, W. M. J., ed. 1997. *Black Athena ten years after*. Holland: Dutch Archaeological and Historical Society.

van Hoof, A. J. L., 1990. *From autothanasia to suicide. Self killing in classical antiquity*. London and New York: Routledge.

van Minnen, P., 2003. "A royal ordinance of Cleopatra and related documents," in Walker and Ashton eds., 35–44.

van Sertima, I., 1984. *Black women in antiquity*. New Brunswick NJ: Transaction Books.

Venit, M., 2002. *Monumental tombs of ancient Alexandria*. Cambridge: Cambridge University Press.

Von Beckerath, J., 1984. *Handbuch der ägyptischen Königsnamen*. Münchner Ägyptologische Studien Heft 20. Munich and Berlin: Deutscher Kunstverlag.

Walker, S., 1985. *Roman burial practices*. London: British Museum Press.

—— 2003a. "From empire to empire," in Walker and Ashton eds., 81–6.

—— 2003b. "From queen of Egypt to Queen of Kings: the portraits of Cleopatra VII" in Bonacasa et al. eds., 508–17.

—— 2003c "Carry-on at Canopus. The Nilotic mosaic from Palestrina and Roman Attitudes to Egypt," in *Ancient Perspectives on Egypt*, edited by R. Matthews and C. Roemer. London: UCL Press, 191–202.

—— 2004. *The Portland Vase*. London: British Museum Press.

Walker, S., and Ashton. S-A., 2003. *Cleopatra reassessed.* The British Museum Occasional Paper 103. London: The British Museum.

—— 2006. *Cleopatra.* London: Bristol Classical Press.

Walker, S., and Higgs, P., eds. 2001. *Cleopatra of Egypt. From history to myth.* London: British Museum Press.

—— 2003. "Cleopatra VII at the Louvre," in Walker and Ashton eds., 71–4.

Warmenbol, E., ed. 2006. *Sphinx.* Brussels: ING and Fonds Mercator.

Waterfield, R., and Stadter, P. A., 1999. *Roman lives: a selection of eight roman lives, Plutarch.* Oxford: Oxford University Press.

Weil Goudchaux, G., 2001. "Cleopatra's subtle religious strategy," in Walker and Higgs eds., 128–41.

Whitehorne, J., 1994. *Cleopatras.* London and New York: Routledge.

Wilkinson, J. G., 1843. *Modern Egypt and Thebes, vol. 1.* London: J. Murray.

Wright, W. C., 1952. *Lives of the Sophists: Philostratus and Eunopius.* London: W. Heinemann.

Yonge, C. D., 1853–54. *Deipnosophistae or Banquet of the Learned of Athenaeus.* London: H.G. Bonn.

Zanker, P., 1990. *The power of image in the age of Augustus.* Ann Arbor: University of Michigan Press.

INDEX

Note: page numbers in italics denote illustrations separated from their textual reference